HEART HEALTHY COOKBOOK FOR BEGINNERS

1500 Days Simple Low Sodium & Low-Fat Recipes to Lower Your Blood Pressure, Cholesterol Levels and Live Longer

TYLER RUIZ

TABLE OF CONTENTS

Introduction 1

Chapter 1: What's The Dash Diet? 3

Chapter 2: Health Benefits Of The Dash Diet 7

Chapter 3: Planning The Dash Diet 11

Chapter 4: Foods To Eat And Avoid 13

Chapter 5: Serving Sizes And Portion Control 19

Chapter 6: Dash Diet Recipes 21

Toast With Almond Butter And Banana 21

Egg Muffin With Berries 21

Healthy "Lox" English Muffin 22

Berries Deluxe Oatmeal 23

Apples And Cinnamon Oatmeal 23

Energy Oatmeal 24

Homemade Granola 24

Warm Quinoa With Berries 25

Fruity Yogurt Parfait 25

Banana Almond Yogurt 26

Open-Faced Breakfast Sandwich 26

Broccoli Omelette 27

Veggie Frittata With Caramelized Onions 27

Veggie Scramble 28

Egg Muffins 29

Veggie Omelette 30

Egg Burrito 31

Whole Grain Pancakes 31

Healthy French Toast 32

Buckwheat Pancakes With Strawberries 33

Lunch 35

Insalata Di Farro (Farro Salad) 35

Asian Quinoa Salad 36

Chicken Pasta Salad 37

Healthy Italian Pasta Salad 37

Balsamic Glaze 38

Basic Vinaigrette 38

Honey Lemon Vinaigrette 39

Lemon Vinaigrette 39

Garlicky Balsamic Vinaigrette 40

Mexican Summer Salad 40

Grilled Romaine Salad With Garlicky Balsamic Vinaigrette 41

Healthy Cobb Salad With Basic Vinaigrette 41

Pomegranate Salad 42

Beet And Heirloom Tomato Salad 43

Caprese Salad With Balsamic Glaze 44

Grilled Tomatillo Salsa 44

Red Mexican Salsa 45

Grilled Chicken With Black Bean Salsa 46

Beef Tacos 46

Curried Chicken Salad Pita Sandwich 47

Chicken Fajita Wraps 48

Asian-Style Lettuce Wraps With Peanut Sauce 48

Italian Veggie Pita Sandwich 49

Turkey Chili 50

Vegetarian Chilli 50

Kale Vegetable Soup 51

Tuna Salad 52

Italian-Style Tuna Salad 53

Chicken In White Wine And Mushroom Sauce 53

Sun-Dried Tomato Basil Pizza 54

Chicken Breasts With Italian Salad 55

Orange Chicken And Brown Rice 56

Grilled Chicken Skewers Marinated In Ginger-Apricot Sauce 56

Chicken Fajitas With Spicy Avocado Sauce 57

Baked Sunflower Seed–Crusted Turkey Cutlets 58

Turkey Meatballs In Marinara Sauce 59

Turkey Meat Loaf 60

Italian Herbed Turkey Cutlets 61

Turkey Roulade With Cider Sauce 61

Stuffed Bell Peppers 63

Sesame Salmon Fillets 63

Spice-Rubbed Salmon 64

Pan-Steamed Orange Roughy 64

Fish Tacos	65
Thai Curried Vegetables	66
Veggie Fajitas	67
Grilled Portobello Burger With Caramelized Onions And Pesto	68
Caramelized Onions	68
Mediterranean Bowl	69
Grilled Veggie Pizza	70
Berry Muesli	71
Veggie Quiche Muffins	71
Turkey Sausage And Mushroom Strata	72
Sweet Millet Congee	73
Sweet Millet Congee	73
Summer Quinoa Bowls	74
Strawberry Sandwich (Halves)	74
Steel Cut Oat Blueberry Pancakes	75
Spinach, Mushroom, And Feta Cheese Scramble	76
Refrigerator Overnight Oatmeal	76
Red Velvet Pancakes With Cream Cheese Topping	77
Perfect Granola	77
Peanut Butter & Banana Smoothie	78
3) Pb + J Yogurt	78
Overnight Oatmeal	79
No Bake Granola Bars	79
Mushroom Shallot Frittata	79
Morning Quinoa	80
Jack-O-Lantern Pancakes	80
Fruit-N-Grain Breakfast Salad	81
Fruit Pizza	82
Directions:	82
Tips:	82
Flax Banana Yogurt Muffins	82
Eggs And Tomato Breakfast Melts	83
Crunchy Avocado "Toast"	83
Broccoli And Cheese Mini Egg Omelets	83
Breakfast Sausage, Potato And Mushroom Strata	84
Pumpkin Cookies	85
Green Smoothie	86

Whole Wheat Pumpkin Pancakes 86
Conclusion 89

INTRODUCTION

A heart-healthy diet, also known as a Dash duet, includes fruits, vegetables, and entire grains. A large part of the Dash diet. Whole grains, lean meats, beef, poultry, and low-fat dairy products. In addition to lowering your blood pressure, it's high in fiber, low in fat, and a great way to lose weight. It's about eating less sodium (salt) and increasing the calcium, magnesium, and potassium intake.

Evidence has shown that both blood pressure and high blood pressure medications can be decreased, and the risk of heart failure, stroke, kidney stones, diabetes, and even some types of cancer minimized. Calcium, protein, fiber, and potassium have all been demonstrated to help lower blood pressure.

Doctors and nutritionists thoughtfully constructed DASH to provide liberal amounts of nutrients for optimal body function. Improved function means better internal body communication so that each body system operates properly and is well connected to other body systems.

This enhanced function and coordination promotes healthy cardiovascular (heart) and digestive (gastrointestinal) systems and contributes to weight management.

CHAPTER 1
WHAT'S THE DASH DIET?

The Dash diet plan is a consequence of clinical trials conducted by scientists from the National Heart, Lung, and Blood Institute (NHLBI). The researchers learned that a diet high in magnesium, potassium, magnesium, fiber, and protein and low in cholesterol and fat might radically reduce hypertension.

The analysis demonstrated that a diet full of fruits, vegetables, and low-fat milk significantly reduced hypertension. Additionally, it revealed that the Dash diet produces rapid outcomes, sometimes in as few as a couple of weeks after starting your diet plan.

The Dash diet highlights three major nutritional elements: magnesium, potassium, and calcium. These dietary supplements are considered to reduce elevated blood pressure. A standard 2,000-calorie diet comprises 500 mg of calcium, 4.7 g of potassium, and 1.2 g of calcium.

Accomplishing the Dash diet

Adhering to the Dash diet is relatively straightforward, and it takes very little time to prepare and choose meals. Foods rich in cholesterol and fats have also been avoided. The dieter is suggested to eat as many veggies, fruits, and cereals as possible.

Considering that the meals you eat on a Dash diet are high in fiber content, it's encouraged that you increase your intake of fat-soluble food to prevent diarrhea and other gastrointestinal issues. It is possible to gradually increase your fiber intake by ingestion yet another serving of fruits and vegetables in every meal.

Grains can also be Great sources of fiber, besides the B complex minerals and vitamins. Whole grains, whole wheat pieces of bread, bran, wheat germ, and low-carb breakfast cereals are several grain products it's possible to eat to maximize your fiber consumption.

You can select the food you eat by looking at the product labels of processed and packaged foods. Search for foods that are lower in fat, saturated fat, cholesterol, and sodium. Meats, chocolates, chips, and fast foods are chief sources of cholesterol and fat, so you should lower your usage.

If you eat beef, limit your consumption to just half daily; this is equal in size to a deck. You might even eat more veggies, rice, cereals, and legumes in your meat dishes. Low-fat or skim milk can be a fantastic source of nourishment minus the surplus cholesterol and fat.

For snacks, you can attempt dried or canned fruits and fresh ones. Additionally, there are healthy snack selections for people on the Dash diet, like graham crackers, unsalted nuts, and low-fat yogurt.

It is Simple to DASH

The Dash diet plan is Popular among several health enthusiasts since it can't require unique recipes and meals. There is no special training, and calorie-counting should be considered as long as you consume fruits and vegetables and lower your consumption of fat and cholesterol-rich food items. The Dash diet plan is a healthy diet program that concentrates on the three significant minerals which can be believed to have a beneficial effect on high blood pressure.

The Dash diet plan is perfect for those that prefer ease and convenience in their eating plans. With scientific evidence to back this up, the Dash diet supplies a tested and proven diet system for those searching for Good health.

Dash diet – Real-life Solutions

The Dietary Plan, Coined the healthier Diet, was made to supply real-life methods for high-blood anxiety by indicating that a dietary plan only regulates nourishment consumption and may not alter the frequent Diet we're used to. Dietary Approaches to stop hypertension or dashboard are targeted at controlling the consumption of fats and sodium to keep the standard blood pressure of somebody. Dash is targeted towards preparing a nutritious diet that makes good foods, preventing people from eating between meals and causing a lack of control over food ingestion. As it stems from an appetite between meals, it becomes more satisfying and less restricting.

The Dash diet Educates people to finish the entire dashboard diet by beginning with stocking the kitchen up using dash-friendly food, preparing dash-friendly recipes, and even performing Dash-friendly exercises. Diet programs indicated by Dash usually contain ingredients full of fiber, fiber, potassium, and magnesium. Dash food diets move low on sugar and sodium and highlight the requirement to consume green leafy fruits and veggies.

For Example, Avocado dip is among the well-known Dash food diets now due to its convenient and affordable preparation. Avocado, a prosperous supply of mono-saturated fat and lutein (antioxidants that help protect vision), is one of the countless fruits that can be highly recommended for a Dash diet plan. Within this recipe, avocado needs to be pitted and mixed with succulent sour cream, milk, and sauce. This dip will likely be eaten together with tortilla chips or chopped lettuce. Out of that particular dish, someone can find an overall total of 65 calories, 2 g protein, 5 g total fat, 4 g carbohydrate, 172 mg potassium, and 3-1 mg calcium. Out of that, we can ensure that an individual has been fed a significant number of crucial nutrients, crucial for keeping up a well-balanced diet that is very good for one's center.

In only 14 days, A Dash diet program will undergo normal blood pressure, with fewer fashions to eat in between foods, and the significant culprit of weight reduction. The Dash diet system teaches people to ascertain the ideal quantity of food ingestion and the essential exercise to execute following age and activity level. Dash instructs and inspires -- certainly one of those crucial reasons folks believe it is easy to stick with a Diet. Additionally, the Diet doesn't require us to provide anything meaningful within our daily Diet. As an alternative, it can help us create a practice of adjusting to modest changes therefore that we can effectively assist ourselves.

CHAPTER 2
HEALTH BENEFITS OF THE DASH DIET

One. You're going to bring down your blood pressure.

This is the primary benefit of adopting the Dash diet, as it is specifically designed to attain this purpose. This Diet is a great option for anyone who currently takes medication to control their blood pressure or for individuals trying to manage prehypertension symptoms better.

According to the Mayo Clinic, after only two weeks, the Dash diet can reduce your blood pressure by a few points–and you could see your systolic blood pressure dropping by eight to 14 points over time–a significant improvement for your overall health and wellness.

Two: You're going to eat more nourishing meals.

This will take some adjustment, especially for people who have never spent much time in the kitchen. But with all the fresh produce you're going to eat and less processed foods in your Diet, you will be able to enjoy much more tasty nutrient-filled meals.

Three: You're going to get lower cholesterol levels.

Due to the nutrients, you'll be consuming from fruits and vegetables, whole grains, nuts, and beans, along with lean cuts of meat and fish, and your minimal consumption of candy and refined carbohydrates, the Dash diet has decreased cholesterol levels. The change continues even with a wider dietary fat variety, which also adds "healthy" cholesterol.

Four: You can just stick with it.

Because this Diet is structured to include delicious foods readily available, it is much easier for dieters to follow. Once you've dedicated yourself to eating the Dash diet, you'll be able to enjoy a change in lifestyle that will be a massive benefit to your overall health and wellness.

Even while dining out, the Dash diet is easy to follow–just be mindful of what foods can hinder your efforts. There are many ways to make the Dash diet work for you, which is a tremendous benefit for anyone seeking to improve their health.

Five: You'll enjoy maintaining a healthy weight.

Whether you're looking to lose/ maintain weight or not, the Dash diet is a perfect option to ensure you can keep up with your target weight once you've achieved it. Adopting a modified version of the Dash diet and sticking to a higher calorie count can help you reach the weight loss goals and keep the weight off; moreover, the healthy food choices in this Diet will ensure that you don't regain any of the importance you've lost.

The Dash diet contains plenty of protein without overloading on carbohydrates, which means you'll enjoy building muscle and improving your metabolism while stopping you from feeling heavy ever. And it's not a short-term diet–it's a new lifestyle, balanced.

Six: You're going to reduce the risk of developing osteoporosis.

Some dietary approaches for osteoporosis prevention and treatment include improved vitamin D and calcium consumption–both in abundance in many of this Diet's items.

Research has shown that "significantly reduced bone turnover" resulted after the Dash diet, which can gradually increase the bone mineral status if continued over a more extended period. The Diet is also abundant in other nutrients strongly correlated with better bone health –magnesium, vitamin C, antioxidants, and polyphenols.

Seven: You have better kidneys.

The Diet's focus on a reduced intake of sodium is also recommended for those at risk of developing kidney disease.

Nonetheless, patients who have already been diagnosed with chronic kidney disease or those on dialysis without a health care professional's advice should not follow the Diet because of the unique requirements for these people.

Eight: You're going to get more protection from certain cancers.

Researchers examined the link between the Dash diet and different types of cancer and found a positive association between decreased salt intake and controlling dietary fat consumption. The Diet is also poor in red meat, which is correlated with colon, rectum, esophagus, liver, lung, prostate, and kidney cancers.

Focusing on fresh produce helps to prevent a variety of cancers, and focusing on low-fat dairy can also lead to lower colon cancer risks.

Nine: You're going to be able to prevent diabetes.

Prevention of insulin resistance, which is linked to hypertension and cardiovascular disease, is aided by the Dash diet. The DASH eating plan helps those predisposed to diabetes prevent or delay the onset of this disease by assisting dietarians to control their sodium intake, consume more fiber and potassium, and maintain a healthy weight.

According to some studies, this impact is even more significant when the DASH plan is implemented as a component of a more comprehensive healthy lifestyle, including diet, exercise, and weight control.

Ten: You're going to avoid feeling hungry.

This Diet will never leave followers with cravings for unhealthy foods, thanks to a high fiber and protein intake–instead, you'll feel satiated all day and look forward to your next balanced, satisfying meal! Also, planning is a good idea, so you can make sure you're on board by taking DASH-approved snacks with you, just in case.

Low-fat diets and cutting carbs may leave you feeling hungry and restricted, but because you are satisfied with the Dash diet, it's much easier to stick to in the long run.

CHAPTER 3

PLANNING THE DASH DIET

One of the benefits of the Dash diet is that it is an eating style against a set of strict rules. That means you can tailor the plan to suit your personal preferences (likes and dislikes). There is no choice but to obey a specific set of rules or go off the board and feel like a failure or loser. Nevertheless, here are some simple tips to help you.

DASH represents a lifestyle change.

More than just habits will need to be altered. Diet to fully enjoy the health benefits of this eating plan. DASH promotes a healthy lifestyle–with plenty of exercise, low consumption of alcohol, and no smoking.

30-60 minutes of exercise daily is recommended. To increase the amount of physical activity. You can either indulge in a particular workout you like or do something fun–clean your house, invest some time in the garden or take the kids and the dog to the park. It's not going to have to be hard work as long as you get your heart rate up and your blood flows.

In addition, for health's sake, you should keep your alcohol use to a minimum. A healthy drinking regimen consists of no more than two drinks per day for women and no more than ten drinks per week for males, in my opinion. Suppose you are taking medication for your blood pressure or other health issues. In that case, it's a good idea to talk to your doctor about your alcohol consumption and ensure every level is appropriate.

Of course, smoking is always harmful to your health, but if you try to lower your blood pressure, it is essential to avoid it. Smoking increases your risk of contracting heart disease or other complications, so make sure your home and office are smoke-free and take action to stop.

Drink more water.

Reduce your intake of sugary fruit juices and sodas. This is a terrific way to stay hydrated and satisfy your thirst without resorting to harmful alternatives. Water is necessary when you have up your fiber intake to prevent constipation and discomfort. As a result of lower sodium intake, you will also store less salt.

In the form of tea, you can also consume additional water -another healthy alternative to sugary beverages or alcohol. Green tea's metabolism-boosting and heart-health-lowering properties make it an ideal addition to any healthy diet. Drinking more water has several health benefits, which is the most effective way to do it.

The change is gradual.

To adopt a healthier lifestyle successfully, it's always a good idea to make small changes one step at a time instead of introducing a significant, dramatic change. That way, you will hardly notice every step and will likely remain committed to your new, healthier lifestyle.

Think about what you're already eating, and seek opportunities to incorporate Dash diet food whenever possible. Vegetables should take more of a central role in the dish than meats or pasta, which would generally take precedence. Cut back on sweets and opt for a piece of fruit instead, or swap your morning swap a natural orange for a glass of orange juice.

With some planning, eating DASH-style will become second nature and be simple to maintain. There's no reason to deviate from this healthy eating plan because it's simple to pack dried fruit or chopped vegetables to enjoy on the move.

Keep an eye on your blood pressure.

This is particularly important if you are not dieting on DASH to lose weight. By checking your blood pressure regularly, you'll be able to track your progress and feel good about the results –giving you a bit of extra motivation to keep up with your diet and lifestyle program to continue to achieve excellent health and wellness. Seeing those numbers dropping is exciting so give yourself the chance to celebrate.

CHAPTER 4

FOODS TO EAT AND AVOID

What follows is a comprehensive list of acceptable meal choices.

WATER

Making sure you get the proper nutrients is a top priority in any diet. Getting adequate water in your system is crucial to ensuring that your body functions properly.

Many people often suffer from dehydration because they do not drink enough water to keep their vital organs filled with safe fluids.

The dehydration perils The average adult body consists of 50 to 65% water. Water loss is more excellent in fatty tissue. as lean tissue, it is harder for your body to retain the moisture needed to help your vital organs function properly. The more fat you have on you.

With so much water already in the body, you would think it would no longer need it, but that's not true. When one part of the body starts getting dry, it decreases the entire fluid flow within the body. It reduces blood pressure by raising blood flow volume and increases blood pressure against the walls of the arteries.

There is a decrease in blood oxygen levels, thus reducing the levels of oxygen that enter the vital organs and body tissue. As this happens, the entire system eventually becomes unbalanced because it doesn't have enough energy to keep the fluids in your body flowing correctly.

How much water are you going to need?

When you work out and sweat, you need to increase the consumption of fluids to compensate for the extra fluid loss. Every 15 minutes, drink 4-8 ounces of water during a workout and another 16 ounces after completing the training to compensate for fluid loss.

Our bodies require 64 fluid ounces of water daily to keep them running efficiently.

If a nurse has ever had trouble getting blood out of your body, try to drink 64 fluid ounces of water every week before the blood works to see if the blood can be drawn easier. 64 Fluid ounces are equivalent to eight-eight glasses of water per day.

[The DASH Diet for Healthy Blood Pressure]

Follow these DASH (Dietary Approaches to Stop Hypertension) guidelines for a healthier, more balanced diet

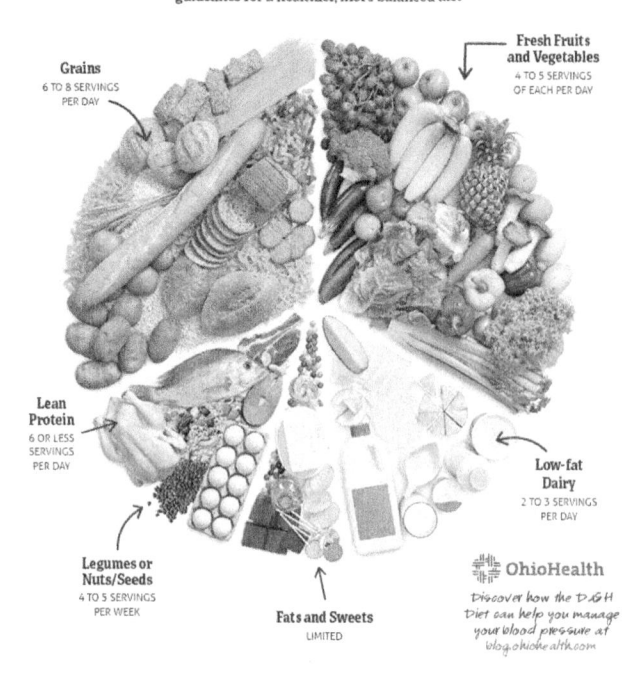

- **Grains** — 6 to 8 servings per day
- **Fresh Fruits and Vegetables** — 4 to 5 servings of each per day
- **Lean Protein** — 6 or less servings per day
- **Low-fat Dairy** — 2 to 3 servings per day
- **Legumes or Nuts/Seeds** — 4 to 5 servings per week
- **Fats and Sweets** — Limited

OhioHealth — Discover how the DASH Diet can help you manage your blood pressure at blog.ohiohealth.com

The best way to get enough liquids to fill what needs to be filled You can get fluids from other sources besides water, but not all juices are created equal, and Certain beverages, if consumed in large quantities, can be detrimental to health. Some drinks, such as sodas and alcoholic beverages, can harm your health. But milk can help you stay hydrated because it's a beautiful source of fluids. Second only to water in importance.

Some of the water intake can also be derived from fruits, vegetables, and the foods you consume. For Example, watermelon is 90 percent water and can help keep your body hydrated.

Water is the center of the Dash diet pyramid. A perfect way to make your H2O consumption more appealing is to apply a drop or two of liquid stevia to your water, along with lemon.

Signs of dehydration

You are dehydrated if you go for eight hours without emptying your bladder. Symptoms of dehydration include dark urine, tiredness, crankiness, moodiness, and headaches. The heart also has to work harder to force blood through your veins when dehydrated.

If it has to compensate for a lack of fluids, the body can react negatively, so ensure you stay hydrated.

Scheduling your fluid intake into your day can occasionally cause an average person to forget to drink water all day. Luckily, some great online alarms and applications might remind you.

During your busy day, don't let a simple thing like forgetting to drink a glass of water cause one more thing to worry about. In addition to relieving stress on your heart, your body will appreciate it if you drink enough water.

Fortified wheat, flour, rice, pasta

This includes fortified cereals, bread, rice, and pasta.

The food group's whole grain types are best because they have more of the essential nutrients, vitamins, and minerals your body needs. These will also produce minor refined chemicals, such as added sugars and colorants.

But how exactly can eating these meals benefit you and your weight loss efforts?

Grainy foods provide energy. Whether a statistical problem or a personal dilemma, the granular food group supports your body's energy level when you exert force through exercise or use your mind to find something out.

Grainy foods keep you feeling full longer. Only half a cup of long-grain rice with a stir-fry will keep you feeling full longer than if your meal doesn't include a serving of whole grains.

Eating breakfast oats is an excellent idea since they are a great source of soluble fiber. Soluble fiber makes the intestines more robust and able to move the by-products.

Bread contains insoluble fiber and is a bulking agent that helps maintain regularity in your body.

Vegetables and Fruits

This next category contains both vegetables and fruits.

The more starchier the vegetable, the sooner it makes you feel full and the longer the feeling of fullness lasts.

Vegetables high in starch convert to sugar during processing and typically contain less water than other types of vegetables. It's easy to overdo it on starchy vegetables, so it's essential to keep an eye on your portion proportions.

The fruit portion is on the other side of the Dash diet pyramid. Healthy, sweet, and tasty fruits will enrich your Diet with water. We also satisfy the innate need for sugar we all have.

Produce is an excellent source of phytonutrients and phytochemicals.

Fruit and vegetables are terrific sources of vitamins and minerals that provide the nutrients your body needs to fight diseases and rejuvenate your system. The source of phytonutrients and phytochemicals for your body comes from that food group.

Phytonutrients and phytochemicals are strength nutrients that protect you against hypertension and various other diseases, including diabetes, stroke, cardiovascular disease, and some malignancies.

Also, fruits and vegetables help you keep your weight healthy by lowering cholesterol and blood pressure.

Eat colorful fruits and vegetables.

Consume a rainbow of fruits and veggies. Consider "rainbow." ROYGBIV is an acronym that can help you remember the colors of the rainbow. It represents the rainbow colors: red, orange, yellow, green, blue, indigo, and violet.

The lighter the colors and the more colors, the more nutrients you get from the fruits and vegetables.

Eating more than the recommended servings.

If you eat more than the recommended daily serving, eat more vegetables first and then migrate to fruits, bearing in mind that some fruits will become sugar in your body after you eat them.

A vegetable or fruit is available where you are deficient in a specific vitamin or mineral that provides the exact nutrient you need to fix the deficiency. Including a vegetable or fruit, you may not usually allow yourself to cover all of your nutrient bases to correct your deficiency naturally rather than with an extra.

Flesh out your culinary skills by learning how to prepare your products correctly.

You must learn how to cook fruits and vegetables to get the most nutrients.

Nutrient loss can vary with fruits and vegetables during the cooking process. Cooking tomatoes, for example, is different from cooking other vegetables because the nutrient values of tomatoes increase the longer they are cooked.

Other vegetables lose much of their nutrient value when cooked for extended periods.

Cooking or burning vegetables at high heat often causes them to lose their nutrient value. On the other hand, it can increase its nutrient value by allowing a garlic clove or onion to rest a few minutes after it has been chopped.

It's essential to do some work on how to cook vegetables and fruits to get the most nutrients out of the food you're cooking.

Milk, yogurt, cheese

It shares meat, poultry, fish, dry beans, and nuts on the ground.

Dairy products;

- Help build stronger teeth and bones
- Support the nervous system in sending and receiving signals
- Aid muscle contraction and relaxation
- Help release hormones and other chemicals in the body
- Help maintain a regular heartbeat. One essential mineral involved in all these body functions is calcium.
- In most dairy products, calcium is a crucial ingredient.

Fish, Poultry, Dry Beans, and Nuts

This category of foods helps the body stay healthy and robust by providing essential nutrients like protein, iron, zinc, and some B vitamins.

Please choose lean meat cuts and remove the skin from meats such as chicken and turkey.

Benefits from this food group

Eggs include a lot of iron and protein; hence they are considered a meat alternative. You should remember that the yolk contains most of the egg's fat when deciding how many eggs to consume at once.

Beans are a low-fat, protein source. We also have a high level of fiber.

Nuts are a decent source of iron and calcium and have high levels of good fat.

Fats, Oils, Sweets, Supplements

Each item in this group of foods shall be used sparingly. Calcium, vitamin D, vitamin B12, and group supplements contradict that.

Most people's diets are deficient in calcium, vitamin D, and vitamin B12; hence the Dash diet pyramid encourages including these nutrients in daily meals. Because of age-related vitamin depletion, taking a supplement containing these vitamins is vital.

Choose your oils and fats wisely.

You need to choose carefully when selecting fats and oils. Omega-3 and omega-6 fatty acids are considered "essential" fatty acids, as they can not be produced by the body alone. They can be obtained only through food. These fats reduce inflammation and protect from heart disease. Such fats are mainly derived from fish, nuts, and some kinds of vegetables.

Processed foods also contain a lot of fats and oils, but these aren't the best kinds of fats and oils to eat.

CHAPTER 5

SERVING SIZES AND PORTION CONTROL

The DASH eating plan emphasizes portion control, consuming a range of foods, and having the right amount of nutrients.

Often the question is not what you consume but how much you eat.

Yes... measuring your food so you can eat healthy portions throughout each food group's day may be a hassle, but it's essential.

And how do you become used to measuring portions every time you eat?

Start by breaking down purchased packets from the supermarket and simply repackaging food in large amounts for you and your families in needed serving sizes.

Say to yourself while repackaging food that you have to make sure you have prepared enough and that you have enough for the leftovers. Then start looking at what you will do with the extra servings you have repackaged.

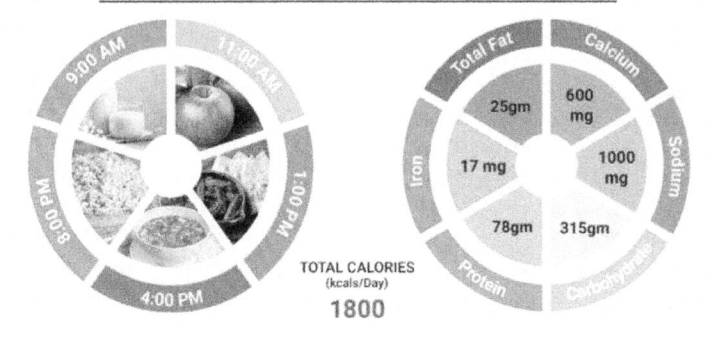

It's fascinating to learn that two very different things are what you need and what you eat.

It was becoming essential to learn to read packages before buying food. Was that food worth a meal? Open your eyes to the value of selecting foods with high nutrients rather than foods that provide little or no nutrients.

Measure snacks into portion size and repackage them into Ziploc bags. It works well because you don't have to do the math when you want a snack. It has already been established.

Break down your meat packets into two, three, and sometimes four different meal plans instead of one or two meals to make extra. Consider snacks to be treats and meals to be meals.

The most effective tip I can provide is to continue your "portion size repackaging attempt" and use the foods existing in your pantry. Fridge and freezer.

Some things will surely surprise you about what a serving size is when you start reviewing serving sizes.

Think about your food and the steps you took to get it on the market. You can find that you can eat more fruit by buying fresh fruit and cutting it yourself.

Why? For what? Since manufacturing involves additives that push up the calories while reducing the serving size. We also need sugar as a preservative when fruits are canned. This reduces the size of the section.

Often, the yogurt would contain additional ingredients when you buy yogurt with natural fruit that the maker had to apply to the yogurt to prevent the fruit from spoiling. This is usually some sugar-based syrup. Buying plain yogurt and adding your fruit to it is a better choice.

CHAPTER 6
DASH DIET RECIPES

Toast with Almond Butter and Banana

- Makes one serving

Ingredients:

- One small banana, sliced
- 1/8 teaspoon ground cinnamon
- Two slices of 100% whole wheat bread
- Two tablespoons of almond butter

How to make

1. Toast the bread, and spread almond butter per slice.
2. Arrange the slices of bananas on top, and sprinkle with cinnamon.

Nutritional value per serving:

Calories 484, total fat 21 grams, saturated 1 gram, polyunsaturated fat 5 grams, monounsaturated fat 11 grams, cholesterol 0 mg, sodium 421 mg, potassium 402 mg, total carbohydrate 56 mg, dietary fiber 12 grams, sugars 21 grams, protein 19 grams.

Egg Muffin with Berries

Makes one serving

Ingredients:

- Four strawberries, thinly sliced
- 1/2 cup blueberries, mashed
- 1 100% whole wheat English muffin, halved
- One tablespoon of low-fat cream cheese

How to make

1. Toast halves of English muffin. Spread the cream cheese on each toasted half evenly, then top with the fruit.

Nutritional value per serving:

Calories 231, Total Fat 4 grams, Saturated Fat 2 grams, Polyunsaturated Fat 0.8 grams, Monounsaturated Fat 1 gram, Cholesterol 8 mg Sodium 270 mg, Potassium 348 mg, Total Carbohydrate 43 grams, Dietary Fiber 8 grams, sugars 11 grams, Protein 8 grams.

Healthy "Lox" English Muffin

Makes two servings

Ingredients:

- Two tablespoons of low-fat cream cheese
- 1 (4-ounce) can of wild salmon in water, no salt added, drained
- 1 100% whole wheat English muffin, halved
- 1/4 teaspoon finely chopped fresh dill
- 1/2 teaspoon fresh lemon juice
- Six thin slices of unpeeled cucumber
- Six thin slices of Roma tomato

How to make

1. Toast half of the English muffin. In the meantime, blend the chopped dill and lemon juice evenly into the cream cheese in a small bowl. Layer the cream cheese mixture evenly over each toasted half of the muffin. To extract the canned liquid, rinse the salmon under running water, and scoop the salmon evenly onto the English muffin half. Suppose the salmon is too big. First, mash with a fork. Top with slices of cucumber and tomato, and sprinkle with chili pepper to taste.

Nutritional value per serving:

One hundred ninety-two calories, 8 grams of fat, saturated fat 2 grams, Polyunsaturated Fat 0.5 grams, Monounsaturated Fat 0.9 grams, Cholesterol 8 mg, Sodium 160 mg, Potassium 241 mg, Total Carbohydrate 18 grams, Dietary Fiber 3 grams, Sugars 0.1 grams, Protein 14 grams.

Protein Bowl

Makes one serving

Ingredients:

- One tablespoon of almond butter
- 3/4 cup low-fat cottage cheese
- 1/2 medium banana, thinly sliced
- 1/4 cup uncooked old-fashioned oats

How to make

1. Combine every ingredient in a small bowl. And enjoy immediately.

Nutritional value per serving:

Calories 346, Total Fat 12 grams, Saturated Fat 2 grams, Polyunsaturated Fat 3 grams, Monounsaturated Fat 7 grams, Cholesterol 7 mg, Sodium 690 mg, Potassium 547 mg, Total Carbohydrate 47 grams, Dietary Fiber 7 grams, Sugars 8 grams.

Berries Deluxe Oatmeal

Makes two servings

Ingredients:

- 3/4 cup mix of blueberries, blackberries, and coarsely chopped strawberries
- 1½ cups unsweetened plain almond milk
- 1/8 teaspoon vanilla extract
- 1 cup old-fashioned oats
- Two tablespoons of toasted pecans

How to make

1. Heat the almond milk and vanilla over medium heat in a small saucepan. When the mixture has started to cook, add the oats and stir for around 4 minutes until most of the drink is absorbed. Stir the berries in. Top with toasted pecans and scoop the mixture into two containers.

Nutritional value per serving:

Total calories 261, saturated fat 10 grams 1 gram, Polyunsaturated Fat 4 grams, Monounsaturated Fat 5 grams, Cholesterol 0 mg, Sodium 115 mg, Potassium 593 mg, Total Carbohydrate 63 grams, Dietary Fiber 11 grams, Sugars 9 grams, Protein 7 grams.

Apples and Cinnamon Oatmeal

Makes two servings

Ingredients:

- One large unpeeled Granny Smith apple, cubed
- 1/4 teaspoon ground cinnamon
- 1½ cups unsweetened plain almond milk
- 1 cup old-fashioned oats
- Two tablespoons of toasted walnut pieces

How to make

1. Bring the milk over medium heat to a boil, then add the oats and apple. Stir until most liquid is absorbed, approximately 4 minutes. Throw in the cinnamon. Scoop the mixture of oatmeal into two plates, then cover with walnuts.

Nutritional value per serving: Calories 377, Total Fat 16 grams, Saturated Fat 4 grams, Polyunsaturated Fat 9 grams, Monounsaturated Fat 4 grams, Cholesterol 15 mg, Sodium 77 mg, Potassium 399 mg, Total Carbohydrate 73 grams, Dietary Fiber 11 grams, Sugars 17 grams, Protein 13 grams.

Energy Oatmeal

Makes one serving

Ingredients:

- Four egg whites, beaten
- 1/8 teaspoon ground cinnamon
- 1/4 cup water
- 1/4 cup of low-fat milk
- 1/2 cup old-fashioned oats
- 1/8 teaspoon ground ginger
- 1/4 cup blueberries

How to make

1. Warm the water and milk in a small saucepan. Pot over medium heat to a simmer. Remove the oats, stirring for about 4 minutes or until most of the liquid is absorbed. Gradually add the beaten egg whites, and stir constantly. Cook for another 5 minutes until the eggs are no longer runny. In the oatmeal mixture, mix the cinnamon and ginger, and scoop the mixture into a bowl. Top with the berries, and immediately serve.

Nutritional value per serving

Calories 270, Total Fat 4 grams, Saturated Fat 2 grams, Polyunsaturated Fat 2 grams, Monounsaturated Fat 2 grams, Cholesterol 5 mg, Sodium 250 mg, Potassium 371 mg, Total Carbohydrate 60 grams, Dietary Fiber 9 grams, Sugars 7 grams, Protein 23 grams.

Homemade Granola

Serves 12 (makes 5 to 6 cups)

Ingredients:

- 1/4 cup brown sugar
- 1/4 cup maple syrup or honey
- 3 cups old-fashioned oats
- 1/4 cup flax seeds
- 1 cup sliced almonds
- 1/2 teaspoon ground cinnamon
- 1/4 teaspoon ground ginger
- 1/4 cup extra virgin olive oil
- 1/2 teaspoon almond extract
- 1 cup golden raisins

How to make

1. Preheat the oven to 250 degrees Fahrenheit. In a large bowl, thoroughly combine the first six ingredients. Mix the maple syrup, honey, butter, and almond extract in a clean, little bowl. Add the liquid components to the dry ingredients and mix thoroughly with a spatula until no dry spots remain.

2. Pour over two slices of greased glass. To achieve an even hue, bake for approximately 1 hour and 15 minutes while stirring every 15 minutes.

3. Break up bits of granola to the desired consistency as you mix. Remove from the oven, and then transfer to a big bowl. Stir in

the raisins so that they are evenly distributed.

Nutritional value per serving:

Calories 262, Total Fat 11 grams, Saturated Fat 2 grams, Polyunsaturated Fat 4 grams, Monounsaturated Fat 7 grams, Cholesterol 0 mg, Sodium 6 mg, Potassium 376 mg, Total Carbohydrate 52 grams, Dietary Fiber 7 grams, Sugars 12 grams, Protein 6 grams

Warm Quinoa with Berries

Makes two servings

Ingredients:

- 1 cup water
- 1/2 cup blackberries
- 1 cup uncooked quinoa
- Two teaspoons of raw honey, optional
- 1 cup unsweetened coconut milk
- Two tablespoons of toasted chopped pecans

How to make

1. Rinse the quinoa (unless pre-rinsed). Over high heat, in a small covered bowl, bring the quinoa, coconut milk, and water to a boil.
2. Reduce to low heat and boil for 10 to 15 minutes or until the liquid is absorbed. Cooked quinoa should be somewhat al dente; it is done when most grains are tender. Are uncoiled, and the unwound germ is visible. Let the quinoa sit in the saucepan for about 5 minutes. Fluff gently into two bowls with a fork and scoop, and top with blackberries, pecans, and honey (if desired).

Nutritional value per serving:

Calories 476, Total Fat 17 grams, Saturated Fat 0.8 grams, Polyunsaturated Fat 3 grams, Monounsaturated Fat 6 grams, Cholesterol 0 mg, Sodium 94 mg, Potassium 221 mg, Total Carbohydrate 70 grams, Dietary Fiber 10 grams, Sugars 7 grams, Protein 14 grams

Fruity Yogurt Parfait

Makes one serving

Ingredients:

- 1/4 cup cubed strawberries
- 1/4 cup cubed kiwifruit
- 1 cup low-fat plain Greek yogurt
- 1/2 cup low-calorie granola
- 1/4 cup blueberries
- One teaspoon of ground flaxseeds or flaxseed meal

How to make

1. In a small glass container or a great tray, scoop half the yogurt. Cover with a thin layer of blueberries, strawberries, kiwifruit,

flaxseed meal, and granola. Layer the remaining yogurt and add the remaining berries, flaxseeds, and granola to the cover.

Nutritional value per serving:

Calories 388, Total Fat 212 grams, Saturated Fat 5 grams, Polyunsaturated Fat 4 grams, Monounsaturated Fat 3 grams, Cholesterol 10 mg, Sodium 98 mg, Potassium 713 mg, Total Carbohydrate 41 grams, Dietary Fiber 7 grams, Sugars 17 grams.

Banana Almond Yogurt

Makes one serving

Ingredients:

- 1/4 cup uncooked old-fashioned oats
- 1/2 large banana, sliced
- One tablespoon of raw, crunchy, unsalted almond butter
- 3/4 cup low-fat plain Greek yogurt
- 1/8 teaspoon ground cinnamon

How to make

1. Smooth the almond butter for about 15 seconds in the microwave. In a bowl, scoop the yogurt, and whisk in the butter, oats, and bananas. Sprinkle over with cinnamon.

Nutritional value per serving:

Calories 337, Total Fat 12 grams, Saturated Fat 3 grams, Polyunsaturated Fat 2 grams, Monounsaturated Fat 6 grams, Cholesterol 8 mg, Sodium 65 mg, Potassium 579 mg, Total Carbohydrate 48 grams, Dietary Fiber 7 grams, Sugars 11 grams, Protein 25 grams.

Open-Faced Breakfast Sandwich

Makes one serving

Ingredients:

- One teaspoon of brown mustard
- One slice of 100% whole wheat bread
- 1 1/2 teaspoons extra virgin olive oil
- Two egg whites, beaten
- 1/2 cup spinach
- Cracked black pepper to taste
- Two thick tomato slices
- One thin slice of low-fat cheddar cheese

How to make

1. Turn the oven or toaster on to 400 degrees Fahrenheit. Put in a small, nonstick range and cook on the stovetop. Cooking oil should be added to a hot pan before any other ingredients. The egg whites when the oil is hot. When cooking, scramble the eggs, add the spinach, and season to taste with pepper.

2. Layer the bread with mustard, add the tomato and scrambled eggs, and top with the cheese. Heat in the oven for about 2 minutes or until the cheese melts.

Nutritional value per serving:

Calories 286, Total Fat 12 grams, Saturated Fat 3 grams, Polyunsaturated Fat 3 grams, Monounsaturated Fat 6 grams, Cholesterol 6 mg, Sodium 515 mg, Potassium 344 mg, Total Carbohydrate 27 grams, Dietary Fiber 4 grams, Sugars 0.1 grams, Protein 20 grams.

Broccoli Omelette

Makes one serving

Ingredients:

- One large clove of garlic, minced
- 1/8 teaspoon chile pepper flakes
- Two egg whites
- One whole egg
- Two tablespoons of extra virgin olive oil
- 1/2 cup chopped broccoli
- 1/4 cup low-fat feta cheese
- Cracked black pepper

How to make

1. Whisk the egg in a small bowl of whites and egg Heat a small nonstick pan over medium heat. Put one tablespoon of the oil in the hot pan and add the broccoli when the oil is hot. Cook for 2 minutes to taste before adding the garlic, chili pepper flakes, and black pepper. Cook for another 2 minutes; remove the broccoli mixture from the saucepan, and put it in a separate bowl.

2. Adjust the heat to medium and toss the remaining tablespoon of oil and the whisked eggs when the oil is hot. When they start bubbling and pulling away from the sides, turn the omelet for about 30 seconds, then scoop the broccoli mixture and feta cheese into half the omelet. In a preheated oven, fold the omelet, cover it with the lid, and let it sit for 2 minutes. Fast service is required.

Nutritional value per serving:

Calories 493, Total Fat 41 grams, Saturated Fat 11 grams, Polyunsaturated Fat 5 grams, Monounsaturated Fat 22 grams, Cholesterol 205 mg, Sodium 984 mg, Potassium 368 mg, Total Carbohydrate 6 grams, Dietary Fiber 3 grams, Sugars 0 gram, Protein 29 grams.

Veggie Frittata with Caramelized Onions

Makes six servings

Ingredients:

For Caramelized Onions;

- 1/4 teaspoon brown sugar
- One tablespoon of extra-virgin olive oil
- One small white onion, thinly sliced
- 1/8 teaspoon cracked black pepper

For Frittata;

- 2 cups spinach
- Four whole eggs

- Five egg whites
- 1/2 cup 1% milk
- 2–3 tablespoons extra virgin olive oil
- 1 1/2 cups chopped zucchini
- One clove of garlic, minced
- 1 cup thinly sliced cremini mushrooms
- 2–3 tablespoons finely chopped fresh basil
- One tablespoon of chopped fresh parsley or one teaspoon of dried parsley
- 1/2 cup shredded low-fat pepper jack cheese
- 1/8 teaspoon sea salt
- Cracked black pepper

How to make

1. Preheat the oven to 350 degrees F.
2. Prepare a medium saucepan over medium heat to caramelize the onions. Stir in the oil and add the onion, sugar, and pepper when the oil is hot. Let the onion "sweat" and stir every few minutes to avoid burning until it is light brown and softened for about 10 minutes. Take the pan off the burner and keep it covered until it's ready to serve.
3. Begin the frittata with a large pan heated over medium heat, and then add the oil. Add the zucchini and cook for about a minute. Add the garlic, and cook for another 2 to 3 minutes before adding the mushrooms, basil, and parsley. Cook vegetables for another minute, and sprinkle on salt and pepper (if you count the salt straight away, the mushrooms should release water, not brown). Mix in, turn off the heat, then add the spinach.
4. Mix the eggs, egg whites, milk, shredded cheese, salt, and pepper in a large bowl.
5. Sprinkle the olive oil spray on a 9-inch circular cake pan. Pour in the ingredients sautéed, then add the egg mixture. Cook the pan for 20–25 minutes until a knife inserted in the center comes clean. (Keep an eye on the timer; eggs can go overcooked rapidly.)

Nutritional value per serving:

Calories 197, Total Fat 14 grams, Saturated Fat 4 grams, Polyunsaturated Fat 2 g, Monounsaturated Fat 7 grams, Cholesterol 135 mg, Sodium 394 mg, Potassium 329 mg, Total Carbohydrate 6 grams, Dietary Fiber 1 grams, Sugars 2 grams, Protein 14 grams.

Veggie Scramble

Makes four servings

Ingredients:

- 1 cup mixed greens (such as collard greens, mustard greens, and kale)
- 1/4 cup chopped red onion
- 1/4 cup chopped red bell pepper
- Two tablespoons water
- One large clove of garlic, minced

- Three whole eggs
- Three egg whites
- 1/8 teaspoon sea salt
- Pinch of cracked black pepper
- 1/2 cup chopped broccoli
- Two tablespoons of extra virgin olive oil

How to make

1. The greens should be washed, dried, and had their thick stems trimmed., and cut the leaves into pieces of 1 inch. Chop the onion, bell pepper, and broccoli into roughly the same size pieces.

2. Heat a large nonstick skillet over medium to high heat and add the oil once the pan is hot. Once the oil is hot, add the greens and sauté for about 3 minutes or until the greens wilt. Pour the water into the saucepan, cover the saucepan with a lid, and steam for 2 to 3 minutes. Remove the top, and whisk in broccoli, pepper bell, onion, and garlic. In the meantime, mix the seeds, egg whites, salt, and pepper in a medium bowl. Once the onion is transparent, add the blend of whisked eggs. Stir to break up and disperse the eggs equally. The eggs are done when they are no longer runny but still look to have slight moisture to them. The dish should be removed from the heat and served immediately.

Nutritional value per serving:

145, Total Fat 11 grams, Saturated Fat 2 grams, Polyunsaturated Fat 2 grams, Monounsaturated Fat 7 grams, Cholesterol 139 mg, Sodium 178 mg, Potassium 196 mg, Total Carbohydrate 4 grams, Dietary Fiber 1 gram, Sugars 0.7 grams, Protein 9 grams.

Egg Muffins

Makes six servings

Ingredients:

- Three whole eggs
- 1/8 teaspoon chile pepper flakes
- 1/4 teaspoon dried oregano
- 4 cups chopped spinach
- 1/2 cup chopped green bell pepper
- 1/2 cup chopped red bell pepper
- Four tablespoons chopped green onion, white ends discarded
- 14 egg whites
- Two tablespoons of finely chopped fresh parsley
- 1/8 teaspoon cracked black pepper
- Pinch of paprika

How to make

1. Make sure your oven is at 375 degrees Fahrenheit. Toss the vegetables together in a big basin, mixing them evenly. Whisk the egg whites, whole eggs, chili pepper flakes, oregano, parsley, pepper, and paprika

together in a separate, large bowl. Spray a muffin tin with a spray of olive oil, making sure the surfaces are also sprayed.

2. In each cup of muffins, scoop the vegetables, filling each about halfway. Pour about 1/3 cup of egg mixture into each cup of muffins so the vegetables do not displace. Place the muffin tin on the oven's middle rack and bake for 25 to 30 minutes until the medium eggs are no longer runny. Immediately remove from the oven to avoid overheating or drying out the eggs. Warmly serve.

Nutritional value per serving:

Calories 93, Total Fat 3 grams, Saturated Fat 1 grams, Polyunsaturated Fat 1 grams, Monounsaturated Fat 1 gram, Cholesterol 93 mg, Sodium 181 mg, Potassium 252 mg, Total Carbohydrate 4 grams, Dietary Fiber 1 gram, Sugars 1 gram, Protein 14 grams.

Veggie Omelette

Makes one serving

Ingredients:

- 1/8 cup shredded low-fat cheddar cheese
- One tablespoon of extra-virgin olive oil
- 1/4 cup coarsely chopped broccoli
- Two tablespoons of chopped red onion
- One clove of garlic, minced
- 1/4 cup chopped zucchini
- Two egg whites
- One whole egg
- 1/8 teaspoon sea salt
- 1/8 teaspoon cracked black pepper

How to make

1. A nonstick pan of adequate size should be heated over moderate heat, and oil should be added after the pan is hot. Add the broccoli and cook for a minute when the oil is hot before adding the onion, garlic, and zucchini. Fall on for 3 to 4 minutes. Whisk the egg whites and whole egg together in a small bowl and season with salt and pepper. Switch the heat to low and add the whisked eggs with the vegetables to the oven, ensuring the pan is tilted so that the eggs cover the vegetables evenly. Turn off the heat after 30 seconds, turn the omelet, and spread the cheese over half of the omelet.

2. One option is to cover the plate or fold the other half over the cheese. Let steam for 1 to 2 minutes or until the cheese is dissolved.

3. Serve straight away.

Nutritional value per serving

Calories 279, Total Fat 20 grams, Saturated Fat 4 grams, Polyunsaturated Fat 3 grams, Monounsaturated Fat 12 grams, Cholesterol 186 mg, Sodium 580 mg, Potassium 313 mg, Total Carbohydrate 6 grams,

Dietary Fiber 2 grams, Sugars 0.8 grams, Protein 20 grams.

Egg Burrito

Makes one serving

Ingredients:

- 1 cup spinach
- 1/8 cup shredded low-fat cheddar cheese
- Cracked black pepper
- 1 100% whole wheat tortilla
- 1/4 cup rinsed and drained canned black beans
- One tablespoon of extra virgin olive oil
- Two tablespoons of chopped white onion
- One clove of garlic, minced
- Two egg whites
- One whole egg
- One tablespoon of chopped fresh cilantro
- 1/4 cup diced Roma tomato
- One tablespoon of prepared low-sodium salsa, optional

How to make

1. A medium-sized skillet is ideal for heating the oil. Cook the onion and garlic for 30 seconds. While waiting, combine egg whites with the entire egg and mix vigorously. Mix in the eggs, cheese, spinach, and seasonings. The eggs should be cooked for about two to three minutes. Take the dish out of the oven immediately.

2. Warm up the tortilla over medium heat in a flat pan. Place the beans in a small saucepan and bring them to a simmer. Set on a plate the warm tortilla, and spoon the beans in a line in the middle of the tortilla. Attach the mixture of vegetables and eggs, and top with cilantro, basil, and salsa (if used). Fold it into a burrito, and enjoy it right away.

3. Nutritional value per serving

4. Calories 460, Total Fat 24 grams, Saturated Fat 4 grams, Polyunsaturated Fat 3 grams, Monounsaturated Fat 12 grams, Cholesterol 189 mg, Sodium 709 mg, Potassium 518 mg, Total Carbohydrate 39 grams, Dietary Fiber 9 grams, Sugars 1 gram, Protein 28 grams.

Whole Grain Pancakes

Makes four servings (about eight 4-inch pancakes)

Ingredients:

- 1/4 cup old-fashioned oats
- Two teaspoons of baking powder
- 1/4 teaspoon sea salt
- One teaspoon of vanilla extract
- One small banana, mashed

- 2 cups unsweetened almond milk
- 1/4 cup unsweetened applesauce
- 1¼ cup whole wheat flour
- 1/2 teaspoon ground cinnamon
- Three tablespoons of brown sugar
- 1/2 cup chopped toasted almonds or walnuts

How to make

1. Bring the wet ingredients together in a medium bowl. Blend the dry ingredients in a separate, more giant bowl. Add the wet ingredients to the dry ingredients, then gently blend properly.
2. Heat a grill pan to medium heat, then cover with a spray of olive oil. To pour the batter onto the pan, use a spoon and cook the pancakes for 2 to 3 minutes. Flip them and cook for about a minute when they start bubbling on top. Remove from heat and stack until all the pancakes are cooked on a covered plate. Serve right away.
3. If desired: Serve with fresh chopped fruit and two teaspoons per cup of maple syrup.

Nutritional value per serving:

Food with a 301-calorie count, 10-gram-total-fat content, 1-gram-saturated-fat content, and 1 gram, Polyunsaturated Fat 2 grams, Monounsaturated Fat 5 grams, Cholesterol 0 mg, Sodium 483 mg, Potassium 372 mg, Total Carbohydrate 55 grams, Dietary Fiber 9 grams, Sugars 14 grams, Protein 9 grams.

Healthy French Toast

Makes four servings

Ingredients:

- One teaspoon of vanilla extract
- 1/4 teaspoon ground nutmeg
- Four egg whites
- One whole egg
- 1 cup unsweetened almond milk
- 1/2 teaspoon ground cinnamon
- 1/2 teaspoon powdered stevia
- Eight slices of whole grain bread (at least 1/2–1 inch thick)

How to make

1. Whisk the egg whites, the whole egg, almond milk, cinnamon, ginger, nutmeg, and stevia together in a shallow bowl. Soak every slice of bread in the mixture for about 1 minute per side so that the bread absorbs the liquid and flavors. Steam the skillet until very hot and coat with olive oil. Place each soaked slice of bread on the griddle pan and cook on each side for about 3 minutes, until browned and crunchy. Serve straight away.
2. If desired: Serve with fresh fruit, yogurt, or two teaspoons of maple syrup per serving.

Nutritional value per serving:

Calories 305, Total Fat 7 grams, Saturated Fat 1

gram, Polyunsaturated Fat 3 grams, Monounsaturated Fat 2 grams, Cholesterol 46 mg, Sodium 438 mg, Potassium 412 mg, Total Carbohydrate 49 grams, Dietary Fiber 6 grams, Sugars 0.3 grams, Protein 15 grams.

Buckwheat Pancakes with Strawberries

Makes six servings

Ingredients:

- One tablespoon of Olive oil
- ½ cup Fat-free milk
- 1/2 cup All purpose flour
- 1/2 cup Buckwheat flour
- One tablespoon of Baking powder
- ½ cup Sparkling water
- 3 cups Fresh strawberries sliced

How to make

1. Whisk the egg whites, the olive oil, and the milk together in a large bowl.
2. Whisk together the all-purpose flour, buckwheat flour, and baking powder in another bowl.
3. Slowly incorporate
4. the dry ingredients into the egg white mixture in between additions of the carbonated water. Blend between each addition until all the ingredients blend into a batter.
5. Place a skillet or nonstick frying pan over medium heat. Spoon 1/2 cup batter pancake into the plate. Once the pancake's surface is smooth and shiny, it's ready. Bubbly, the edges are a light golden brown, usually taking approximately 2 minutes. After 1–2 minutes, flip and continue cooking to achieve a golden brown color on the underside. Make another batch of pancakes using the remaining batter.
6. The pancakes are moved to individual plates. Using 1/2 cup of sliced strawberries to top each. Serve it.

Nutritional value per serving:

Total carbohydrate 24grams, Dietary fiber 3 grams, Sodium 150 mg, Saturated fat - trace, Total fat 3 grams, Cholesterol - trace, Protein 5 grams, Monounsaturated fat 2 grams, Calories 143.

LUNCH

The following lunch recipes are chock-full of fruits, vegetables, and nutritious protein, providing plenty of midday meal choices. Don't be tempted to skip lunch to reduce caloric intake! This will cause your blood sugar to plummet and slow down your metabolism. Eating healthy food at regular intervals guarantees blood sugar and a consistent burning of metabolic calories. The instant lunch comes around; you notice that you're super hungry. Make sure you get enough protein at breakfast and lunchtime.

Insalata di Farro (Farro Salad)

Makes six servings

Ingredients:

- Two tablespoons of finely chopped fresh basil
- 1/8 teaspoon dried marjoram
- Juice of 1/2 lemon
- 1/2 cup roasted chopped zucchini (see below)
- 2 cups Italian semi-pearled farro
- 8 ounces chopped fresh mozzarella cheese
- 1 (8-ounce) jar of roasted red peppers, chopped
- Two tablespoons of finely chopped fresh parsley
- Two tablespoons of extra virgin olive oil
- 1/4 teaspoon sea salt
- 1/2 teaspoon cracked black pepper
- For the Roasted Zucchini;
- Four tablespoons of balsamic vinegar
- Two zucchini cut lengthwise into 1/4-inch slices
- Four tablespoons of extra virgin olive oil
- 1/4 teaspoon cracked black pepper
- 1/2 teaspoon dried Italian herbs

How to make

1. For best results, set the oven temperature to 400 degrees Fahrenheit while roasting the zucchini. Zucchini. Coat a cookie sheet with olive oil spray, and place the sliced zucchini on it. Add olive oil and balsamic vinegar, and sprinkle with pepper and dried herbs. Cook on the middle rack for 8-10 minutes or until the zucchini wrinkles and is tender to the touch.

2. To prevent the farro from sticking, bring a big saucepan of water to a boil and add a drizzle of olive oil. Farro needs 20-30 minutes in a saucepan of boiling water. Or until it reaches the desired texture. After washing the farro in a colander, transfer it to a big basin.

3. Bring together the roasted zucchini and all

other ingredients in the cooked farro. Toss well, and then serve right away. Doing this warm dish can cause the mozzarella to melt, but it can also be eaten chilled.

Nutritional value per serving:

Calories 189, Total Fat 8 grams, Saturated Fat 4 grams, Polyunsaturated Fat 0.3 grams, Monounsaturated Fat 2 grams, Cholesterol 22 mg, Sodium 757 mg, Potassium 195 mg, Total Carbohydrate 24 grams, Dietary Fiber 4 grams, Sugars 0.5 grams, Protein 13 grams.

Asian Quinoa Salad

Makes six servings

Ingredients:

- 1/2 cup chopped red bell pepper
- 1/8 teaspoon chile pepper flakes
- 1/2 teaspoon grated orange zest
- Two tablespoons of finely chopped fresh Thai basil
- 2 cups uncooked quinoa
- 4 cups low-sodium vegetable broth
- 1 cup cooked, shelled edamame
- 1/4 cup chopped green onion
- 1½ teaspoons finely chopped fresh mint
- 1/2 cup chopped carrot
- Juice of 1/2 orange
- One teaspoon of sesame seeds
- One tablespoon of sesame oil
- One tablespoon of extra virgin olive oil
- 1/8 teaspoon cracked black pepper

How to make

1. Rinse the quinoa (unless pre-rinsed). Over high heat, in a small covered kettle, bring the quinoa and vegetable broth into a roiling mass.
2. Raise heat to a simmer and bring to a low boil. a simmer. 10 to 15 minutes, or until most of the liquid has been absorbed. When most grains have uncoiled, and the unwound germ is visible, the quinoa is done cooking and should be served al dente slightly. Let the quinoa sit for some 5 minutes in the covered bowl. Fluff the cooked quinoa gently with a fork and move to a large bowl, then mix in the remaining ingredients. Serve and cool to room temperature. You can also eat the dish chilled.
3.

Nutritional value per serving:

Calories 331, Total Fat 10 grams, Saturated Fat 0.7 grams, Polyunsaturated Fat 2 grams, Monounsaturated Fat 3 grams, Cholesterol 0 mg, Sodium 103 mg, Potassium 95 mg, Total Carbohydrate 50 grams, Dietary Fiber 6 grams, Sugars 7 grams, Protein 11 grams.

Chicken Pasta Salad

Makes six servings

Ingredients:

- 1/2 cup chopped celery
- 1/2 cup low-fat plain Greek yogurt
- 8 ounces whole wheat penne pasta
- 1 (6-ounce) boneless, skinless chicken breast
- 1 cup halved seedless red grapes
- 1/4 cup walnut pieces
- One tablespoon of red wine vinegar
- 1/2 teaspoon cracked black pepper
- 1/8 teaspoon sea salt

How to make

1. Get the water in a large saucepan, boiling first. Then drizzle olive oil to keep the pasta from sticking. Add the pasta, stirring once, to the boiling water and cook for 8 to 10 minutes or until al dente.
2. Wrap the pasta.
3. Trim the fat off the chicken, if any, while the pasta is cooking, and cut it into small cubes. Fill a separate medium pot with water over high heat, and bring it to a boil. Add the chicken cubes (water will cover them), then boil for 5 to 6 minutes.
4. Drain the rice, as well as the chicken. Combine the pasta and chicken with the remaining ingredients in a large bowl, then combine well. Refrigerate 20 to 30 minutes before serving.
5. You can substitute canned wild salmon or tuna for cooked chicken. Just be sure to look for fish released in water, not oil, with no added salt.

Nutritional value per serving:

115 Calories, 4 g Fat, 2% Saturated Fat 0.5 grams, Polyunsaturated Fat 3 grams, Monounsaturated Fat 0.6 grams, Cholesterol 16 mg, Sodium 84 mg, Potassium 165 mg, Total Carbohydrate 11 grams, Dietary Fiber 2 grams, Sugars 3 grams, Protein 10 grams

Healthy Italian Pasta Salad

Makes four servings

Ingredients:

- One bunch of coarsely chopped fresh basil
- Four tablespoons of extra virgin olive oil
- 4 cups whole wheat penne pasta
- 1/4 cup toasted pine nuts
- 2 cups halved cherry tomatoes
- 1 cup chopped fresh mozzarella cheese
- Pinch of sea salt
- 1/8 teaspoon cracked black pepper

How to make

1. Boil a big pot of water, adding an olive oil drizzle to prevent sticking the pasta. Add the pasta, stirring once, to the boiling water and cook for 8 to 10 minutes or until al dente.

2. Squeeze the pasta.

3. Prepare a big, flat pan over medium-high prepare toast the pine nuts. Remove the nuts of the pine and mix often to avoid burning. Toast for about 2 minutes or until butter smells from the nuts; on the outside, they are light brown. Immediately remove them from the oven.

4. The pasta should be served immediately after it has been cooked and tossed with the remaining ingredients in a large bowl. The moist pasta melts the cheese slightly.

Nutritional value per serving:

Calories 388, Total Fat 15 grams, Saturated Fat 5 grams, Polyunsaturated Fat 3 grams, Monounsaturated Fat 6 grams, Cholesterol 22 mg, Sodium 254 mg, Potassium 72 mg, Total Carbohydrate 45 grams, Dietary Fiber 5 grams, Sugars 4 grams, Protein 18 grams.

Balsamic Glaze

Makes six servings

Ingredients:

- 2 cups balsamic vinegar

How to make

1. Heat the balsamic vinegar in a large saucepan for 25 to 30 minutes. Just prepare it, and don't let it cool. Dip a wooden spoon into the glaze to test; if you run your finger over the spoon's back, it should leave a clean line behind. Drizzle, heat, and stack the salads, entrées, and desserts in a squeeze bottle.

Nutritional value per serving:

Calories 85, Total Fat 0 grams, Saturated Fat 0 grams, Polyunsaturated Fat 0 grams, Monounsaturated Fat 0 grams, Cholesterol 0 mg, Sodium 53 mg, Potassium 0 mg, Total Carbohydrate 21 grams, Dietary Fiber 0 grams, Sugars 0 grams, Protein 0 grams.

Basic Vinaigrette

Makes six servings

Ingredients:

- 1/2 cup extra virgin olive oil
- 1/8 teaspoon sea salt
- 1/2 teaspoon Dijon or brown mustard
- 1/2 teaspoon reduced-sugar marmalade (any fruit flavor)
- 1/4 cup balsamic vinegar (sweet) or red wine vinegar (acidic)
- Cracked black pepper

How to make

1. Whisk together the mustard, marmalade, and vinegar in a small bowl. Drizzle very slowly

in the oil, then start to whisk together. (Constant whisking emulsifies oil and vinegar, throwing the droplets into each other, producing a thick dressing.) Add salt and pepper. Store in an airtight jar or container unless used immediately.

2. Note: The base for the homemade Vinaigrette is recommended to consist of 1 part vinegar or another acid, such as lemon, lime, or orange juice, and two parts oil.

Nutritional value per serving:

It has 19 grams of fat and dish, 9 of which are saturated. and calories 170 3 grams, Polyunsaturated Fat 3 grams, Monounsaturated Fat 13 grams, Cholesterol 0 mg, Sodium 62 mg, Potassium 1 mg, Total Carbohydrate 3 grams, Dietary Fibre 0 grams, Sugars 0.8 grams, Protein 0 grams

Honey Lemon Vinaigrette

Makes six servings

Ingredients:

- 1/8 teaspoon sea salt
- 1/8 teaspoon cracked black pepper
- Juice of 3 lemons (about 1/4 cup)
- One tablespoon honey
- One teaspoon of chopped fresh thyme
- 1/2 cup extra virgin olive oil

How to make

1. Whisk the lemon juice, honey, thyme, salt, and pepper together in a small bowl. Drizzle very slowly in the oil, and continue to whisk together. If not to be used, instantly store it in an airtight container or jar.

Nutritional value per serving:

Calories 173, Total Fat 19 grams, Saturated Fat 3 grams, Polyunsaturated Fat 3 grams, Monounsaturated Fat 13 grams, Cholesterol 0 mg, Sodium 49 mg, Potassium 15 mg, Total Carbohydrate 4 grams, Dietary Fiber 0.1 grams, Sugars 3 grams, Protein 0.1 grams.

Lemon Vinaigrette

Makes six servings

Ingredients:

- 1/8 teaspoon sea salt
- Juice of 3 lemons (about 1/4 cup)
- One tablespoon of Dijon mustard
- One teaspoon of chopped fresh parsley
- 1/8 teaspoon cracked black pepper
- 1/2 cup extra virgin olive oil

How to make

1. Whisk the lemon juice, mustard, parsley, salt, and pepper together in a small container. Drizzle very slowly in the oil, and continue to whisk together. For future use, store in an airtight container or jar.

Nutritional value per serving:

Calories 102, Total Fat 10 grams, Saturated Fat 1 gram, Polyunsaturated Fat 3 grams, Monounsaturated Fat 7 grams, Cholesterol 0 mg, Sodium 79 mg, Potassium 81 mg, Total Carbohydrate 9 grams, Dietary Fiber 3 grams, Sugars 3 grams, Protein 0.7 grams.

Garlicky Balsamic Vinaigrette

- 1/2 cup extra virgin olive oil
- Pinch of dried oregano
- 1/2 teaspoon Dijon mustard
- One large clove of garlic, finely minced
- 1/2 teaspoon reduced-sugar raspberry marmalade
- 1/4 cup balsamic vinegar
- 1/8 teaspoon sea salt
- Cracked black pepper

How to make

1. Whisk the mustard, garlic, marmalade, and vinegar together in a tiny bowl. Drizzle in the oil very slowly, and continue to whisk together. Add the salt and pepper and the oregano.

Nutritional value per serving:

Calories 66, Total Fat 7 grams, Saturated Fat 1 gram, Polyunsaturated Fat 1 gram, Monounsaturated Fat 5 grams, Cholesterol 0 mg, Sodium 90.1 mg, Potassium 3.7 mg, Total Carbohydrate 1.2 grams, Dietary Fiber 0.1 grams, Sugars 0 grams, Protein 0 grams.

Mexican Summer Salad

- 1 1/2 cups of cucumber, sliced and unpeeled
- White onion, cut very thinly, about a quarter cup
- A Quarter Cup of Fresh Lime Juice
- Three heads of romaine lettuce, chopped
- 5 Roma tomatoes, chopped
- 1/8 cup extra virgin olive oil
- Sea salt
- Cracked black pepper

How to make

1. Combine the lettuce, tomato, cucumber, and ointment in a large bowl. Pour over the salad with the lime juice and oil, then toss well.
2. Season with salt and pepper to taste.

Nutritional value per serving

Saturated Fat 3.5 grams, Total Fat 5 grams, Calories 78 0.7 grams, Polyunsaturated Fat 0.6 grams, Monounsaturated Fat 3 grams, Cholesterol 0 mg, Sodium 61 mg, Potassium 405 mg, Total Carbohydrate 9 grams, Dietary Fiber 2 grams, Sugars 0.2 grams, Protein 2 grams.

Grilled Romaine Salad with Garlicky Balsamic Vinaigrette

Makes four servings

Ingredients:

- 1/2 cup halved cherry tomatoes
- 1/4 cup chopped walnuts
- Two tablespoons of olive oil
- One head of romaine lettuce (about 12 leaves)
- 1/4 cup feta cheese
- Garlicky Balsamic Vinaigrette recipe is as above

How to make

1. Take the stem and cut it off from the leaves. Romaine, and wash and dry. Heat a grill to medium-high, brush oil on both sides, and place on the grill. Watch carefully and frequently turn, as the leaves can wax fast. Replace the leaves once char marks are clear, and place three leaves on four individual plates. Finish the grilled lettuce with the walnuts, tomatoes, and cheese. Drizzle the balsamic Vinaigrette with two tablespoons, and serve.

Nutritional value per serving:

Calories 152 (218), Total Fat 14 grams (21 grams), Saturated Fat 3 g (4 g), Polyunsaturated Fat 4 grams (5 grams), Monounsaturated Fat 6 grams (11 grams), Cholesterol 8 mg (8 mg), Sodium 109 mg (199 mg), Potassium 126 mg (130 mg), Total Carbohydrate 5 grams (6 grams), Dietary Fiber 1 gram (1 gram), Sugars 1 gram (1 gram), Protein 3 grams (3 grams).

Note that numbers in parentheses are figures with Vinaigrette

Healthy Cobb Salad with Basic Vinaigrette

Makes four servings

Ingredients:

- 1/2 large cucumber, sliced
- 1/2 (15-ounce) can of kidney beans, rinsed and drained
- Four slices of turkey bacon
- 5 cups spinach
- 1 cup sliced cremini mushrooms
- 1/2 cup shredded carrot
- One large avocado, pitted, peeled, and chopped
- 1/3 cup crumbled blue cheese
- The Basic Vinaigrette recipe is as above

How to make

1. A nonstick pan of adequate size should be heated at moderate heat and sprinkled with olive oil. Add the turkey bacon, cook for 5 to 6 minutes until brown, then flip and continue cooking.

2. Remove it from the cutting board and rest it on it. Crumble by hand, or chop the cooled turkey bacon.

3. Place the spinach on a large platter for serving. Then arrange in neat rows atop the spinach mushroom, carrot, cucumber, kidney beans, avocado, blue cheese, and turkey bacon. Serve with Vinaigrette by the side.

4. Note:

5. With its strong flavor, just a little blue cheese goes a long way, which is why a modest amount of this high-fat ingredient is included.

6. For variety, substitute feta cheese for blue cheese. It's milder in flavor and considerably lower in fat.

Nutritional value per serving:

Calories 232 (402),Total Fat 14 grams (33 grams), Saturated Fat 4 grams (7 grams), Polyunsaturated Fat 1 gram (4 grams), Monounsaturated Fat 5 grams (18 grams), Cholesterol 23 mg (23 mg), Sodium 612 mg (674 mg), Potassium 797 mg (798 mg), Total Carbohydrate 19 g (21 grams), Dietary Fiber 9 grams (9 grams), Sugars 1 grams (2 grams), Protein 11 grams (11 grams).

Pomegranate Salad

Makes four servings

Ingredients:

- 1/2 cup thinly sliced Anjou pears, thinly sliced
- 4 cups arugula
- One large avocado, pitted, peeled, and chopped
- 1/2 cup thinly sliced fennel
- 1/4 cup pomegranate seeds

How to make

1. Using a large basin, mix all the ingredients, adding, last of all, the pomegranate seeds. Oil and vinegar, or any other dressing you choose, can be used as a side. Prepare the fennel by slicing it very thinly, preferably with a mandoline.

Per-serving nutritional value

There are 106 calories in this. There are 7 grams of fat, 0.9 grams of which are saturated. Polyunsaturated Fat 0.9 grams, Monounsaturated Fat 4 grams, Cholesterol 0 mg, Sodium 15 mg, Potassium 414 mg, Total Carbohydrate 12 grams, Dietary Fiber 4 grams, Sugars 4 grams, Protein 2 grams.

Beet and Heirloom Tomato Salad

Ingredients:

- 1/4 cup toasted walnut pieces
- 1/4 cup crumbled goat cheese
- 1 cup cooked, thinly sliced beets
- 6 cups mixed greens
- 1 cup green heirloom tomato, sliced and cut in fourths
- 1/4 cup balsamic vinegar
- Cracked black pepper to taste

How to make

1. Prepare the beets with the green stems cut off and the beets washed. Cut off the beet's very top and bottom, then peel off its thick skin. Over medium heat, steam the beets for about 15 minutes in a small pot with 1/2 to 1 cup of water. When done, let it cool before slicing it into quarters like heirloom tomatoes.

2. In a large salad bowl, put the mixed greens, and top with the beets, tomatoes, walnuts, and goat cheese. Drizzle with balsamic vinegar, then grind the rim with cracked black pepper.

Nutritional value:

One hundred sixty-eight calories, 10 grams of fat, 3 grams of saturated fat. Polyunsaturated Fat 4 grams, Monounsaturated Fat 2 grams, Cholesterol 11 mg, Sodium 257 mg, Potassium 643 mg, Total Carbohydrate 156 grams, Dietary Fiber 2 grams, Sugars 6 grams, Protein 8 grams.

Green Salad with Lemon Vinaigrette

Makes four servings

Ingredients:

- One teaspoon of dried oregano
- Ten black pitted olives, rinsed, drained, and chopped
- 4 cups chopped romaine leaves (about two large heads of lettuce)
- 1/2 cup halved cherry tomatoes
- 1/2 cup rinsed and drained, coarsely chopped canned artichoke hearts
- 1/4 cup low-fat feta cheese
- Eight tablespoons of Lemon Vinaigrette
- The recipe for lemon Vinaigrette is as above

How to make

1. Toss everything together in a big salad dish, and toss well. Serve each plate with two lemon vinaigrette tablespoons on the side.

2. Both artichoke hearts and olives often come in very salty brines. Look for those in water

instead of oil, with no added salt.

Nutritional value per serving:

Calories 69 (171), Total Fat 4 grams (13 grams), Saturated Fat 2 grams (3 grams), Polyunsaturated Fat 1 gram (4 grams), Monounsaturated Fat 0.3 grams (3 grams), Cholesterol 2 g (8 g), Sodium 311 mg (401 mg), Potassium 255 mg (259 mg), Total Carbohydrate 7 g (7 g), Dietary Fiber 3 grams (4 grams), Sugars 0.8 grams (0.8 grams), Protein 3 grams (3 grams).

Caprese Salad with Balsamic Glaze

Makes six servings

Ingredients

- Five tablespoons of extra virgin olive oil
- Five large beefsteak tomatoes, cut into 1/2-inch slices
- One bunch of fresh basil
- One pound of fresh buffalo mozzarella cheese, sliced to a thickness of one-fourteenth of an inch
- Five tablespoons of Balsamic Glaze
- Pinch of sea salt
- 1/8 teaspoon cracked black pepper

How to make

1. Arrange tomatoes sliced on a large platter. Top with a large basil leaf and a slice of mozzarella on each side. Drizzle over the platter with balsamic glaze and oil, then sprinkle with salt and pepper.
2. The balsamic Glaze recipe is as above.

Nutritional value per serving:

Calories 334 (419), Total Fat 24 grams (24 grams), Saturated Fat 9 grams (9 grams), Polyunsaturated Fat 2 grams (2 grams), Monounsaturated Fat 12 grams (12 grams), Cholesterol 43.8 mg (44 mg)Sodium 408 mg (461 mg), Potassium 70 mg (70 mg), Total Carbohydrate 11 grams (32 grams), Dietary Fiber 1 gram (1 gram), Sugars 4 grams (4 grams), Protein 19 grams (19 grams).

Grilled Tomatillo Salsa

Makes 16 servings

Ingredients:

- Two cloves garlic
- 3/4 cup fresh cilantro
- 20 tomatillos, husked and washed
- 1/2 small white onion, cut into large pieces
- One sizeable whole jalapeño chile pepper, stem cut off
- 1 cup water
- 1/2 teaspoon sea salt

How to make

1. Heat the barbecue grill to medium-high heat. Put the whole tomatillos right on the grill.

Watch them closely, rotate them every 2 to 3 minutes, and turn around on all sides to blacken them. When they darken or burn, it's okay, as it will add to their flavor. They're done when picked up with tongs when they feel soft and squishy.

2. Cover the cooked tomatillos in a bowl to continue steaming while the rest of the tomatillos finish grilling. After grilling all the tomatillos, leave them in the covered pot for 15 to 20 minutes until they are completely cooled. They must release liquid when cooling to produce the salsa, which may be used in place of water or mixed with water.

3. Cook the onion, chili pepper, and garlic in a small pot over high heat until they start to brown. After 2 minutes, add the liquid tomatillo or oil-water mixture, and cover. Simmer for about 5 minutes or till the onion is easily inserted into a fork.

4. Move the mixture of onions, tomatillos (first scraping any rough cores and leaving the skin on), and cilantro in batches to a blender, combine at low speed, and then fast until smooth. Salt single lots to taste. Mixed sets are stored in an airtight container.

Nutritional value per serving:

Calories 15.4, Total Fat 0.4 grams, Saturated Fat 0.1 grams, Polyunsaturated Fat 0.2 grams, Monounsaturated Fat 0.1 grams, Cholesterol 0 mg, Sodium 1 mg, Potassium 119 mg, Total Carbohydrate 3 grams, Dietary Fiber 0.9 grams, Sugars 2 grams, Protein 0.5 grams

Red Mexican Salsa

Makes 12 servings

Ingredients:

- 1/2 cup water
- 3/4 cup fresh cilantro
- 20 dried red chiles/chiles de arbol
- One large clove of garlic
- 1/2 white onion, cut into large pieces
- Two large Roma tomatoes, cut into large pieces
- 1/4 teaspoon sea salt

How to make

1. On high heat, use a wide skillet. Add the chiles, garlic, onion, and tomatoes to the saucepan directly without oil. Once the tomato skins and chilies begin to blacken, remove the chilies from the two skillets, and submerge them in a shallow pan of water.

2. Cover, and simmer to soften the chilies for 8 to 10 minutes.

3. Once the chiles have been softened, pass the cooked ingredients to a blender along with the cilantro. Blend at low speed and cover the top with a kitchen towel to allow steam to escape, but the salsa will not blast out of

the blender's lid. Season with to-taste salt. Caution: Hot salsa!

Nutritional value per serving:

Calories 10, Total Fat 0.1 g Saturated Fat 0 gram, Polyunsaturated Fat 0 gram, Monounsaturated Fat 0 gram, Cholesterol 0 mg, Sodium 132 mg, Potassium 54 mg, Total Carbohydrate 2 grams, Dietary Fiber 0.3 grams, Sugars 0 gram, Protein 0.2 grams.

Grilled Chicken with Black Bean Salsa

Makes four servings

Ingredients:

- Juice of 1 large lime
- Juice of 1/2 orange
- 1/8 teaspoon sea salt
- Black beans, 2 cups, drained and rinsed from a can
- One large Granny Smith apple, chopped
- 1/2 small red onion, finely chopped
- One serrano chile pepper, seeded and finely chopped
- Two tablespoons of chopped fresh cilantro
- 1/8 teaspoon cracked black pepper
- Four boneless, skinless chicken breasts

How to make

1. Combine all ingredients (excluding salt, pepper, and chicken) in a large bowl to make the salsa. Refrigerate to let the flavors meld for at least an hour.
2. Heat a grill or grill pan to medium-high heat. Season with salt and pepper over the chicken breasts. Place them on the grill and cook for 4 to 6 minutes per side or until each is no longer pink in the center. Break the salsa over the breasts, and eat.

Nutritional value per serving:

Calories 251, Total Fat 1 gram, Saturated Fat 0.2 grams, Polyunsaturated Fat 0.3 grams, Monounsaturated Fat 0 gram, Cholesterol 55 mg, Sodium 232 mg, Potassium 431 mg, Total Carbohydrate 30 grams, Dietary Fiber 9 grams, Sugars 5 grams, Protein 31 grams.

Beef Tacos

Makes four servings

Ingredients:

- 1/4 teaspoon cracked black pepper
- 3/4 cup chopped Roma tomato
- One teaspoon chopped jalapeño chile pepper (seeded for less heat)
- Two tablespoons of extra virgin olive oil
- 1/2 cup chopped white onion, divided
- 1 cup chopped red bell pepper
- One large clove of garlic, minced

- 1/2 pound 95%-lean ground beef
- 1/2 teaspoon dried oregano
- Four tablespoons of chopped fresh cilantro
- Juice of 1/2 lime
- 8 (6-inch) corn tortillas
- Four radishes, thinly sliced

How to make

1. A medium-heat process must be involved in heating oil in a big skillet. Add the onion, bell pepper, and garlic to a quarter cup and heat for 30 seconds. After that, add the ground beef and use a spatula to break up any significant bits. Stir in the oregano and black pepper as the meat cooks.

2. Combine the remaining 1/4 cup of chopped onion, tomato, chili pepper, cilantro, and lime juice in a separate bowl to form a salsa topping. Mix to be evenly incorporated, and set aside.

3. Warm the tortillas in a flat pan over medium heat. Place two tortillas on four individual plates, scoop the beef mixture onto the tortillas, fold and serve on top with salsa and sliced radishes.

Nutritional value per serving:

Polyunsaturated Fat 2 grams, Monounsaturated Fat 5 grams, Cholesterol 33 mg Sodium 73 mg, Potassium 318 mg, Total Carbohydrate 31 grams, Dietary Fiber 5 grams, Sugars 2 grams, Protein 16 grams.

Curried Chicken Salad Pita Sandwich

Makes four servings

Ingredients:

- 1½ teaspoons red wine vinegar
- One teaspoon of curry powder
- 1/4 teaspoon ground cinnamon
- 4 100% whole wheat pitas (with pockets)
- 2 (6-ounce) boneless, skinless chicken breasts
- 1/2 cup chopped carrot
- 1/3 cup chopped green onion
- 1/4 cup golden raisins
- 3/4 cup low-fat plain Greek yogurt
- Two romaine lettuce leaves, chopped
- Eight heirloom tomatoes, sliced
- 1/4 cup chopped toasted almonds

How to make

1. Trim the chicken off fat, and split the breasts into fourths. Fill with water in a medium pot and bring to a boil. Add the chicken, and cook for 8 to 10 minutes until the centers are orange. Strain the chicken, then set it aside for cooling. Combine the carrot, green onion, and raisins in a medium-sized bowl. Shred the chicken with two forks, then add to the dish. Add yogurt, vinegar, curry, and cinnamon, then mix well. Chill for 30 minutes.

2. Warm up the pitas in a large skillet over low heat, then cut them in half and split them open. Add salad mixture to each pita pocket, top with almonds and serve.

Nutritional value per serving:

340 calories, 7 grams of fat, 1 gram of saturated fat, Polyunsaturated Fat 1 gram, Monounsaturated Fat 3 grams, Cholesterol 51 mg, Sodium 297 mg, Potassium 553 mg, Total Carbohydrate 41 grams, Dietary Fiber 7 grams, Sugars 3 grams, Protein 32 grams

Chicken Fajita Wraps

Makes four servings

Ingredients:

- One large green bell pepper, thinly sliced
- One large red bell pepper, thinly sliced
- 4 100% whole wheat tortillas
- Three tablespoons of extra virgin olive oil
- 2 (6-ounce) boneless, skinless chicken breasts
- One teaspoon of dried oregano
- 1/8 teaspoon sea salt
- 1/8 teaspoon black pepper
- 1/2 large white onion, thinly sliced
- Black beans, one cup's worth (drained and washed) from a can
- 1 cup shredded romaine lettuce
- Four tablespoons of low-fat plain Greek yogurt

How to make

1. To prepare, heat the oil in a large skillet under moderate heat. While the pan heats, strip the fat from the chicken breasts, slice them about 1/4 inch thick lengthwise, and cut the longer pieces in half. Season with salt, pepper, and oregano. Add the chicken to the oven, then sauté for 5 to 6 minutes until the details are no longer pink in the middle. Take the chicken from the saucepan, then set it aside. Add the onion and bell peppers to the same pan, then sauté for about 4 minutes, or until onions are tender but still retain some texture. Warm the tortillas up over low heat in a flat pan.

2. Divide the tortillas into the black beans, lettuce, rice, sautéed peppers, and onions. Place yogurt on top, cover, and serve.

Nutritional value per serving:

Calories 366, Total Fat 14 grams, Saturated Fat 2 grams, Polyunsaturated Fat 2 grams, Monounsaturated Fat 8 grams, Cholesterol 35 mg, Sodium 557 mg, Potassium 317 mg, Total Carbohydrate 40 grams, Dietary Fiber 9 grams, Sugars 3 grams, Protein 24 grams.

Asian-Style Lettuce Wraps with Peanut Sauce

Makes four servings

Ingredients:

- 1 cup bean sprouts

- 1/2 cup chopped red bell pepper
- 2 cups uncooked red quinoa
- 4 cups low-sodium vegetable broth
- Eight large butter lettuce leaves
- 1 cup chopped snow peas (in thirds)
- 1/2 cup shredded carrot
- Four teaspoons of sesame seeds

How to make

1. Rinse the quinoa (unless pre-rinsed). Over high heat in a sizable covered pot, bring the quinoa and vegetable stock to a boil.

2. Simmer until the liquid is absorbed on low heat. It is done when most grains are uncoiled and the unwound germ is visible; cooked quinoa should be slightly al dente. Let the quinoa sit for some 5 minutes in the covered pot. Gently fluff up with a fork.

3. Place each lettuce leaf with 1/2 cup of cooked quinoa. In a medium bowl, blend the snow peas, bean sprouts, bell pepper, and carrots. Stir until the peanut butter dissolves, and bring to a simmer over low heat. Pour the sauce over the chopped vegetables into the bowl. Toss well, and spoon evenly in each lettuce leaf on top of the quinoa. Sprinkle the sesame seeds over the veggies, then serve.

Nutritional value per serving:

Calories 486, Total Fat 15 grams, Saturated Fat 1 gram, Polyunsaturated Fat 2 grams, Monounsaturated Fat 2 grams, Cholesterol 0 mg, Sodium 77 mg, Potassium 135 mg, Total Carbohydrate 73 grams, Dietary Fiber 10 grams, Sugars 10 grams, Protein 17 grams.

Italian Veggie Pita Sandwich

Makes one serving

Ingredients:

- 1 (1/4-inch-thick) slice of fresh mozzarella cheese
- 1 (1/4-inch-thick) slice of heirloom tomato
- 1 100% whole wheat pita (with pocket)
- One tablespoon of prepared pesto
- 1/2 cup arugula
- 1/4 cup roasted red pepper (about two large pieces from a jar)
- 1/8 teaspoon cracked black pepper

How to make

1. Warm up the pita in a skillet on both sides over low heat. Remove from heat, halve the pita, split it open, and spread pesto inside. Top with arugula, onion, cheese, and red pepper. Top with black peppers.

Nutritional value per serving:

Polyunsaturated Fat 0.4 gram, Monounsaturated Fat 0.1 gram, Cholesterol 8 mg, Sodium 379 mg, Potassium

210 mg, Total Carbohydrate 23 grams, Dietary Fiber 4 grams, Sugars 2 grams, Protein 6 grams.

Turkey Chili

Makes eight servings

Ingredients:

- 1/2 pound lean ground turkey
- 1/2 cup chopped red onion
- Three medium cloves of garlic, minced
- 2 cups chopped fresh tomatoes
- 2½ cups chopped zucchini
- One tablespoon of chili powder
- 1/4 teaspoon ground cumin
- 1/2 teaspoon dried parsley
- 1/2 teaspoon dried oregano
- 1/2 teaspoon dried basil
- 3 cups low-sodium chicken broth
- Two tablespoons of extra virgin olive oil
- 1/8 teaspoon ground black pepper
- 1/8 teaspoon sea salt
- 1/2 cup shredded low-fat cheddar cheese for garnish
- 1/4 cup chopped fresh cilantro, for garnish

How to make:

1. Heat the oil in a broad sauté pan.
2. Place the beef, onion, and garlic on the table. Cook for 6 minutes until cooked, stirring and breaking turkey chunks with a spatula.
3. Place the remaining ingredients into a 6-quarter crock pot, then add the cooked turkey mixture. Mix well, cover, and cook for 4 hours on high or 8 hours on low. Serve in cups, then top with cilantro and cheese.
4. If a crock pot is unavailable, cook over low heat in a large pot with a lid on the stove. As the chili may get hotter and the liquid can evaporate faster on the stovetop than in a crock pot, check regularly and add broth where appropriate.

Nutritional value per serving:

Calories 266, Total Fat 11 grams, Saturated Fat 2 grams, Polyunsaturated Fat 1 gram, Monounsaturated Fat 4 grams, Cholesterol 42 mg, Sodium 497 mg, Potassium 556 mg, Total Carbohydrate 24 grams, Dietary Fiber 7 grams, Sugars 3 grams, Protein 19 grams.

Vegetarian Chilli

Makes eight servings

Ingredients:

- 2 (15-ounce) cans of low-sodium diced tomatoes
- One tablespoon of chili powder

- 1/2 teaspoon ground cumin
- 1/2 teaspoon dried parsley
- 1/2 teaspoon dried oregano
- 1/2 teaspoon dried basil
- 1/8 teaspoon black pepper
- 1/8 teaspoon sea salt
- 3/4 cup low-sodium vegetable broth
- Three tablespoons of extra virgin olive oil
- 1/2 large red onion, chopped
- Three large cloves of garlic, minced
- Four small zucchinis, chopped
- 1/2 cup chopped red bell pepper
- 1/2 cup chopped yellow bell pepper
- Eight tablespoons of low-fat plain Greek yogurt
- One large avocado, pitted, peeled, and thinly sliced
- Four tablespoons of chopped fresh cilantro

How to make

1. Heat the oil and add the onion and garlic. Stir in the zucchini and bell peppers after 3 to 4 minutes. Stir in the vegetables until the onion is translucent.
2. Move the remaining ingredients to a 6-quarter crock pot. Cook for 4 to 6 hours at low, then add water if necessary. Serve with two slices of avocado and cilantro in bowls and finish with yogurt.
3. When no crock pot is available, cook over low heat in a large pot with the lid on the stove. If possible, check often and add a little water, as the chili may get hotter, and the liquid can evaporate more easily on the stovetop than in a crock pot.

Nutritional value per serving:

Calories 257, Total Fat 10 grams, Saturated Fat 1 gram, Polyunsaturated Fat 3 grams, Monounsaturated Fat 6 grams, Cholesterol 0.2 mg, Sodium 426 mg, Potassium 851 mg, Total Carbohydrate 35 grams, Dietary Fiber 11 grams, Sugars 5 grams, Protein 10 grams

Kale Vegetable Soup

Makes six servings

Ingredients:

- 1/2 teaspoon dried oregano
- 1/4 teaspoon chile pepper flakes
- 1/8 teaspoon sea salt
- 1-quart low-sodium vegetable broth
- Two tablespoons of extra virgin olive oil
- Three medium carrots, sliced
- Three small sweet potatoes, diced
- One large yellow onion, chopped
- Three large cloves of garlic, minced
- Two small yellow zucchini, cubed

- 1 (14-ounce) can of low-sodium diced tomatoes
- 1/2 teaspoon fresh thyme, chopped
- 2 cups coarsely chopped kale

How to make

1. Heat the oil pot. Add the carrots, sweet potatoes, onion, and garlic and cook for about 4 to 5 minutes until they begin softening. Add the zucchini, oregano, chili pepper, and salt, and cook for 1 minute. Stir in the water with milk, canned tomatoes, and thyme. Bring to a boil and cook for 10 minutes. Add the kale and beans, then simmer until the kale is wilted and the sweet potatoes are tender, for 10 minutes more. Serve warm.

Nutritional value per serving:

Calories 195, Total Fat 5 grams, Saturated Fat 0.8 grams, Polyunsaturated Fat 0.9 grams, Monounsaturated Fat 3 grams, Cholesterol 0 mg, Sodium 297 mg, Potassium 613 mg, Total Carbohydrate 29 grams, Dietary Fiber 7 grams, Sugars 5 grams, Protein 6 grams.

Tuna Salad

Makes four servings

- 2 (6-ounce) cans of albacore tuna in water, no salt added, drained
- One teaspoon of brown mustard
- Three tablespoons of low-fat plain Greek yogurt
- 1/4 cup chopped celery
- 1/2 jalapeño chile pepper, seeded and chopped
- 1/4 cup diced Roma tomato
- 1/4 cup chopped red onion
- 1/8 teaspoon cracked black pepper
- One small avocado, thinly sliced

How to make

1. Combine the celery, chili pepper, tomato, and onion in a medium bowl. Blend the salmon, mustard, yogurt, and pepper until well mixed. Finish the avocado slices in the salad, and serve.

Nutritional value per serving:

Calories 162, Total Fat 7 grams, Saturated Fat 0.9 grams, Polyunsaturated Fat 0.8 grams, Monounsaturated Fat 4 grams, Cholesterol 38 mg, Sodium 241 mg, Potassium 318 mg, Total Carbohydrate 32 grams, Dietary Fiber 6 grams, Sugars 1 gram, Protein 21 grams

Italian-Style Tuna Salad

Makes four servings

Ingredients:

- Four tablespoons of finely chopped fresh parsley
- Juice of 1 lemon
- 2 (5-ounce) cans of albacore tuna in water, no salt added, drained
- 1/2 cup chopped Roma tomato
- 1/4 cup chopped red onion
- Four tablespoons of extra virgin olive oil
- 1/8 teaspoon cracked black pepper

How to make:

1. Place the ingredients in a bowl, then stir to be evenly absorbed. Let rest before serving for 30 minutes.
2. Calories 205, Total Fat 15 grams, Saturated Fat 2 grams, Polyunsaturated Fat 2 grams, Monounsaturated Fat 10 grams, Cholesterol 38 mg, Sodium 192 mg, Potassium 94 mg, Total Carbohydrate 4 grams, Dietary Fiber 2 grams, Sugars 0 gram, Protein 19 grams

Chicken in White Wine and Mushroom Sauce

Makes four servings

Ingredients:

- 4 - 4 ounces each of Boneless Skinless Chicken breast
- Two tablespoons of Olive oil
- Four thinly sliced Shallots
- 1/4 pound thinly sliced Fresh Mushrooms
- One tablespoon of All-purpose (plain) flour
- 1/4 cup White Wine
- 1/2 cup low-sodium Chicken Stock
- One tablespoon of Fresh Rosemary (or one teaspoon of dried rosemary)
- Two tablespoons of chopped Fresh Parsley

How to make

1. Place the chicken breasts in a sealed Ziploc bag with a mallet, pound, or use a rolling pin to flatten them.
2. Cut the chicken, and lengthwise cut each piece in half. Return to Ziploc bag and cool down until firm.
3. Have two frying pans ready to cook when the chicken is firm by placing one teaspoon of olive oil in each pan.
4. Add the flour and wine to a small bowl, then whisk until all the lumps are gone. Set sideways. Switch all frying pans to moderate heat. Add the chicken breast to frying pan number one. Sauté the shallots in frying pan number two for about 3 minutes.
5. Return to the number one frying pan and turn the chicken breast over.
6. Return to the number two frying pan and add shallots with the mushrooms. Stir for

another 2 minutes while the two sauté together.

7. Get the bowl of blended wine and starch. Whisk a few times, then spill over the shallots and mushrooms. Remove the stuffed chicken and stir.

8. The chicken in the first casserole should have a lovely brown shade on both sides and be cooked with no remaining white. Heat and plate clean.

9. Add to the saucepan and stir in the mushroom and shallot, making sure it thickens nicely. Switch off the chicken mixture over the burner and bowl.

10. Sprinkle with parsley, then serve hot piping.

Nutritional value per serving:

Total fat 9 g, Calories 239, Protein 28 grams, Cholesterol 66 mg, Total carbohydrate 6 grams, Dietary fiber 0.5 grams, Monounsaturated fat 5 grams, Saturated fat 1 gram, Sodium 98 mg

Sun-Dried Tomato Basil Pizza

Makes four servings

Ingredients:

- One crust 12-inch prepared pizza crust purchased or made from a mix
- 4 Garlic cloves
- ½ cup fat—free ricotta cheese
- ½ cup chopped dry-packed sun-dried tomatoes
- Two teaspoons of Dried basil
- One teaspoon Thyme
- Red pepper flakes
- Parmesan cheese

How to make

1. Coat a 12-inch circular pizza baking pan and spray gently.

2. Reconstitute sun-dried tomatoes before use. Let stand for 5-10 minutes or until pliable and soft. Chop and drain.

3. Place the pizza crust in a pie-baking pizza saucepan. Arrange garlic, onions, and tomatoes on the pizza's crust. Sprinkle the basil and the thyme over the pizza uniformly.

4. Bake on the oven's lowest rack until the pizza crust turns brown and the toppings are dry, about 20 minutes.

5. Split the pie into even eight slices and serve straight away.

6. Place the red-flaked pepper jar and parmesan jar for individual use.

Nutritional value per serving:

Total fat 2 grams, Calories 179, Protein 8 grams, Cholesterol 8 mg, Total carbohydrate 32 grams, Dietary fiber 2 grams, Monounsaturated fat 0.5 grams, Saturated fat - trace, Sodium 276 mg

Chicken Breasts with Italian Salad

Makes four servings

Ingredients:

For the salad:

- 1 cup diced fresh mozzarella cheese
- 1/4 cup extra virgin olive oil
- 1/4 cup balsamic vinegar
- 1 cup cherry tomatoes, halved
- Two small zucchini, sliced thinly and cut into half moons
- 1/8 teaspoon sea salt
- Cracked black pepper
- 4 cups arugula
- Two tablespoons of chopped fresh basil
- For the chicken:
- 1/8 teaspoon sea salt
- Cracked black pepper
- One teaspoon of dried oregano
- 1/2 teaspoon minced fresh rosemary
- 1/2 teaspoon garlic powder
- Four boneless, skinless chicken breasts

How to make

1. The tomatoes, zucchini, and cheese are mixed in a medium bowl to make the salad. Stir in the oil, vinegar, salt, and pepper, and blend well. Cover and refrigerate until ready for the chicken. (Arugula and basil are to be added later.) Trim the fat off the chicken breasts. Combine the oregano, rosemary, garlic powder, salt, and pepper in a small bowl to taste and blend well. Sprinkle the mixture over the chicken breasts on both sides. Heat a large casserole over medium heat and sprinkle with olive oil. Once the oil is heated, add chicken breasts, two at a time to avoid overeating. Cook per breast for 4 to 6 minutes per side or until the center is pink.

2. When cooking the second batch of chicken, remove the salad from the refrigerator, add the arugula and basil, then toss well.

3. Once the chicken has been fried, let it rest for about 2 minutes, then slice each breast onto the diagonal, making chicken strips. Set the salad on a plate, and top it with shredded chicken.

Nutritional value per serving:

Calories 400, Total Fat 24 grams, Saturated Fat 8 grams, Polyunsaturated Fat 3 grams, Monounsaturated Fat 13 grams, Cholesterol 88 mg, Sodium 549 mg, Potassium 360 mg, Total Carbohydrate 9 grams, Dietary Fiber 2 grams, Sugars 2 grams, Protein 38 grams.

Orange Chicken and Brown Rice

Makes two servings

Ingredients:

- 1/4 teaspoon cracked black pepper
- 1/2 teaspoon grated orange zest
- 1/4 teaspoon grated lemon zest
- Juice of 1/2 orange
- 2 (4-ounce) boneless, skinless chicken breasts
- One tablespoon of sesame oil
- One tablespoon of extra virgin olive oil
- 1/2 cup coarsely chopped shiitake mushroom
- 1/4 cup chopped white onion
- One large clove of garlic, minced
- 4 cups spinach
- 1/4 teaspoon ground ginger
- 1 cup cooked brown rice

How to make

1. Trim the fat from the breasts of the chicken, then cut the chicken into small cubes. Heat the olive oil and the sesame oil over medium heat in a medium oven. Add the mushroom, onion, and garlic and cook for 1 minute; then add the chicken, then season with the pepper, ground ginger, orange zest, and lemon zest. Cook for about 4-5 minutes until the chicken has browned, then add the orange juice.

Nutritional value per serving:

Calories 334, Total Fat 15 grams, Saturated Fat 2 grams, Polyunsaturated Fat 4 grams, Monounsaturated Fat 8 grams, Cholesterol 55 mg, Sodium 282 mg, Potassium 498 mg, Total Carbohydrate 25 grams, Dietary Fiber 4 grams, Sugars 5 grams, Protein 27 grams

Grilled Chicken Skewers Marinated in Ginger-Apricot Sauce

Makes four servings

Ingredients:

- 4 (4-ounce) chicken breasts, cut into 1-inch cubes
- Three large red bell peppers, cut into 1-inch pieces
- Two large white onions, cut into 1-inch pieces
- Six apricots were pitted and cut into 1-inch pieces

For Marinade

- Four tablespoons of apple cider vinegar
- 1/4 cup extra virgin olive oil
- One heaping tablespoon of reduced-sugar apricot marmalade
- 1/2 teaspoon sesame oil
- 1½ teaspoons finely chopped fresh ginger or 3/4 teaspoon ground ginger
- One tablespoon of Dijon mustard or brown mustard
- One large clove of garlic, chopped

How to make

1. In a zip-top bag, add the cubed chicken, pour in the marinade, squeeze the air out of the bag and seal tightly. Perform the mixture by hand into the chicken by shifting around the bag and contents. Chill for at least 2 hours.
2. Soak 12 large wooden skewers in water, then cut the peppers, onions, and apricots into pieces of similar size.
3. Skewer the rice, pepper, onion, and apricot bits and alternative ingredients. Grill the skewers on a hot grill or pan until the chicken is no longer pink in the center. (If you use a charcoal grill or gas grill, remove the grill cover so the chicken does not dry out.)

Nutritional value per serving:

Calories 314, Total Fat 16 grams, Saturated Fat 2 grams, Polyunsaturated Fat 2 grams, Monounsaturated Fat 10 grams, Cholesterol 55 mg, Sodium 357 mg, Potassium 403 mg, Total Carbohydrate 21 grams, Dietary Fiber 4 grams, Sugars 10 grams, Protein 25 grams.

Chicken Fajitas with Spicy Avocado Sauce

Makes four servings

Ingredients:

For the sauce;

- Juice of 1/2 lemon
- 1/2 small serrano chile pepper
- One large avocado, pitted, peeled, and cut in fourths
- 1/2 cup low-fat plain Greek yogurt
- 1/4 cup water
- 1/8 teaspoon sea salt
- 1/8 teaspoon cracked black pepper

For Fajitas;

- 4-ounce boneless, skinless chicken breasts cut into 1/2-inch- thick strips

- 1/8 teaspoon sea salt
- 1/8 teaspoon cracked black pepper
- One teaspoon of dried oregano divided
- Two large green bell peppers, cut into 1/2-inch-thick strips
- Two large yellow bell peppers, cut into 1/2-inch-thick strips
- One large white onion, cut into 1/2-inch slivers
- Two large cloves of garlic, minced
- Eight corn tortillas
- 1/4 teaspoon ground cumin
- Three tablespoons of extra virgin olive oil
- Two large red bell peppers, cut into 1/2-inch-thick strips

How to make

1. Place all the ingredients in a blender for the sauce, and blend until smooth. Deposit aside.
2. Season, the chicken for the fajitas with salt, pepper, cumin, and half oregano. Heat the oil. Add the chicken, then cook for 4 to 5 minutes. Add the bell peppers, the onion, the garlic, and the dried oregano remaining.
3. Warm up the tortillas over low heat in a skillet. Scoop the mixture of chicken and veggie with avocado sauce into each tortilla and drizzle. Fold over the tortilla, and drink.
4. Serve with toppings, such as black beans, shredded lettuce, low-fat cheese, and salsa.

Nutritional value per serving:

Calories 463, Total Fat 20 grams, Saturated Fat 3 grams, Polyunsaturated Fat 3 grams, Monounsaturated Fat 12 grams, Cholesterol 55 mg, Sodium 415 mg, Potassium 839 mg, Total Carbohydrate 46 grams, Dietary Fiber 10 grams, Sugars 4 grams, Protein 32 grams.

Baked Sunflower Seed–Crusted Turkey Cutlets

- Makes four servings
- 1/4 teaspoon paprika
- 1/4 teaspoon cayenne pepper
- 2 (6-ounce) skinless, boneless turkey breasts
- 1 1/2 cups unsalted sunflower seeds
- 1/4 teaspoon ground cumin
- Two tablespoons coarsely chopped fresh parsley
- 1/4 teaspoon cracked black pepper
- 1/3 cup whole wheat flour
- Three egg whites

How to make:

1. Preheat to 400 ° F in the oven.
2. Place the turkey between the sheets of plastic wrap and pound to a thickness of about 1/2.

Cut out half of each pounded breast. The sunflower seeds, cumin, parsley, paprika, cayenne, and pepper are mixed in a food processor. Pulse until the kernels are heavily cut. Pour the mixture of seeds over a flat plate. Whisk the egg whites in a vast, relatively shallow bowl. In this order, create a dredging assembly line: flour plate, egg cup, and seed mixing board. Dip every breast into the flour and dredge it lightly on both sides. Then dip it into the eggs' whites and the seed mixture onto the plate. Press firmly down and brush the seed mixture on both sides of the turkey. Coat a cookie sheet with a spray of olive oil, and put on the sheet the crusted breasts. Serve straight away.

Nutritional value per serving;

Calories 408, Total Fat 26 grams, Saturated Fat 3 grams, Polyunsaturated Fat 16 grams, Monounsaturated Fat 5 grams, Cholesterol 37 mg, Sodium 377 mg, Potassium 467 mg, Total Carbohydrate 20 gram, Dietary Fiber 7 grams, Sugars 1 gram, Protein 29 grams

Turkey Meatballs in Marinara Sauce

Makes four servings

Ingredients:

- 1 pound lean ground turkey
- 1/2 small red onion, finely chopped
- Two large cloves of garlic, minced
- Three tablespoons finely chopped fresh parsley
- 1/8 teaspoon cracked black pepper
- One large egg
- 1/4 cup whole wheat bread crumbs
- 1/8 teaspoon sea salt
- Four tablespoons of extra virgin olive oil
- 1 (16-ounce) jar of low-sodium marinara sauce
- 1/2 cup low-fat feta cheese
- 1/2 teaspoon chile pepper flakes
- 1/8 teaspoon ground cumin
- 1/2 teaspoon dried Italian herbs (premixed, or use thyme, rosemary, oregano, parsley, and basil)

How to make

1. Preheat to 375 ° F in the oven.
2. Combine all ingredients except for the butter, marinara, and feta. Blend well by hand until the meat contains ingredients, and be careful not to overmix. Roll the mixture into the size of small balls.
3. Steam a large skillet over medium-high steam without sticking. Once it is heated, add the oil in five batches and the meatballs.

Sear on each side (don't cook through all the way), and put in an ovenproof dish. Once all the meatballs are sewn and put into the container, top with the marinara sauce and cover with foil. Bake for about 20-25 minutes.

4. Clear from the oven, and heat to 400 ° F.

5. Remove the foil from the pot, feta over the meatballs, and bake for 4 minutes. Immediately remove, and serve.

Nutritional value per serving:

Polyunsaturated Fat 4 grams, Monounsaturated Fat 14 grams, Cholesterol 143 mg, Sodium 1485 mg, Potassium 852 mg, Total Carbohydrate 32 grams, Dietary Fiber 6 grams, Sugars 2 grams, Protein 32 grams.

Turkey Meat Loaf

Makes six servings

Ingredients:

- One teaspoon of Dijon mustard
- One teaspoon of Worcestershire sauce
- One slice of 100% whole wheat bread, crust removed and torn into small pieces
- 1/4 cup low-sodium chicken stock
- 1 1/4 pounds lean ground turkey
- One large egg
- 1/4 cup finely chopped onion
- 1/4 cup finely chopped bell pepper
- 1/4 cup chopped fresh parsley
- One teaspoon horseradish
- 1/2 teaspoon sea salt
- 1/4 teaspoon black pepper

How to make:

1. Preheat your oven to 300 degrees F. Place all ingredients in a large bowl, and combine until the ingredients are evenly mixed with your hands, be careful not to overmix. A 9-by-5-inch loaf pan (or deep baking dish) is lightly greased with olive oil spray. Shape the meat mixture into a sandwich, then place it in the oven. Bake uncovered for an hour or so.

2. When baked, remove the meatloaf from the oven and allow it to cool for about 10 minutes. Drag a butter knife along the sides to extract it from the saucepan, turn it into a large serving dish and slice it to serve.

Nutritional value per serving:

Calories 152, Total Fat 7 grams, Saturated Fat 2 grams, Polyunsaturated Fat 0.2 grams, Monounsaturated Fat 0.5 grams, Cholesterol 91 mg, Sodium 319 mg, Potassium 68 mg, Total Carbohydrate 4 grams, Dietary Fiber 0.6 grams, Sugars 0.8 grams, protein 19 grams.

Italian Herbed Turkey Cutlets

Makes four servings

Ingredients:

- 1/2 teaspoon cracked black pepper
- 4 (4-ounce) boneless, skinless turkey cutlets
- Three small cloves of garlic, minced
- Two tablespoons chopped fresh rosemary
- Two tablespoons of chopped fresh parsley
- 1 1/2 teaspoons chopped fresh sage
- Grated zest of 1 large lemon
- 1 cup low-sodium vegetable broth

How to make

1. Preheat to 375 ° F in the oven.
2. Blend the garlic, rosemary, parsley, basil, and pepper in a small bowl. Rub a generous amount of the blend of herbs on both sides of each cutlet. In a 9-by-13-inch baking dish, put the turkey cutlets, top with lemon zest, and add the vegetable broth to the pot. Remove the foil to brown the tops of the cutlets during the last 5 minutes of baking. Remove and serve immediately from the oven.

Nutritional value per serving:

Polyunsaturated Fat 0.3 grams, Monounsaturated Fat 0.6 grams, Cholesterol 49 mg, Sodium 1188 mg, Potassium 373 mg, Total Carbohydrate 7 grams, Dietary Fiber 1 gram, Sugars 5 grams, Protein 19.6 grams

Turkey Roulade with Cider Sauce

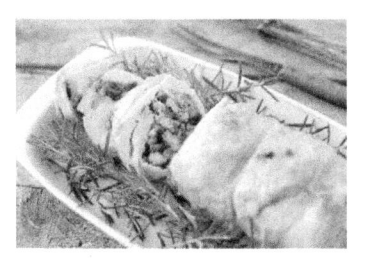

Makes four servings

Ingredients:

1. 1 (2-pound) skinless, boneless turkey breast
2. 1/4 teaspoon sea salt
3. Five tablespoons of extra virgin olive oil divided
4. 1/2 cup diced white onion, divided
5. Four cremini mushrooms, thinly sliced
6. 2 cups spinach
7. Three medium cloves of garlic, minced
8. 1/2 cup white wine
9. 1 1/2 cups low-sodium chicken broth divided

10. 1/3 cup dried cranberries
11. Three slices of 100% whole wheat bread, cut into 1/2-inch squares
12. 1/2 cup chopped almonds
13. One sizeable fresh sage leaf, finely minced
14. One teaspoon of chopped fresh thyme
15. One teaspoon of chopped fresh parsley
16. 1/2 teaspoon cracked black pepper
17. For cider sauce;
18. 1 1/2 cups cider, divided
19. One tablespoon cornstarch
20. 1/2–1 cup roasting liquid from turkey

How to make

1. Preheat to 375 ° F in the oven.
2. Heat some oil in a large pan over medium heat to make the filling for the roulade. Add 1/4 cup of the onion with the mushrooms, spinach, and garlic and cook until translucent. Add the white wine, then boil to let the alcohol cook for about a minute. Remove 1/2 cup of broth and the cranberries together. Attach the bread, almonds, and fresh herbs once the broth is heated (but not boiling). Cook, then simmer for 2 to 3 minutes. The filling should not be too soupy.
3. Butterfly the turkey breast by putting your hand flat on top of it and cutting it sideways into the breast, ensuring you don't completely cut it through. Open the butterflied breast, and place it between two plastic wrap sheets. Flatten the turkey with a 1/2 "thick mallet. Add salt and pepper to both sides. Spread the turkey filling, holding it in the direction of the middle. Roll the turkey breast up and secure it in three positions (middle and two ends) with kitchen twine. Take the pan where the filling was cooked to high heat and sear the rolled turkey breast on both sides for 3 to 4 minutes per side to a brown color.
4. Drizzle in a medium roasting pan the remaining three tablespoons of oil in. Remove the remaining onion and broth. Place the turkey in the middle of the saucepan, cover with foil and bake for about 1 hour.
5. Apply 3/4 cup of cider to the turkey-searing pan, and scrape the bottom of the pan to mix in the juices. Whisk the remaining cider with the cornstarch in a small bowl and add to the plate. Boil for 2 to 3 minutes, until the sauce gets thick.
6. Once the turkey is removed from the oven, add up to 1 cup of the roasting juices to the cider sauce, and mix well. Hold the turkey covered and let the turkey rest for ten minutes. Take the turkey from the roasting pan, then cut the twine off. Slice the turkey, then top with cider sauce on each slice.

Nutritional value per serving:

Calories 518, Total Fat 14 grams, Saturated Fat 2

grams, Polyunsaturated Fat 3 grams, Monounsaturated Fat 9 grams, Cholesterol 80 mg, Sodium 2,788 mg, Potassium 314 mg, Total Carbohydrate 44 grams, Dietary Fiber 4 grams, Sugars 9 grams, Protein 50 grams

Stuffed Bell Peppers

Makes four servings

Ingredients:

- 1/2 pound 95%-lean ground beef
- 1 cup chopped zucchini
- One tablespoon of chopped fresh parsley
- Two tablespoons of extra virgin olive oil
- 1/2 small white onion, chopped
- Two small cloves of garlic minced
- 1/2 cup chopped carrot
- 1/4 teaspoon dried thyme
- 1/4 teaspoon dried basil
- Four large red bell peppers
- 2 cups low-sodium marinara sauce

How to make

1. Preheat to 350 ° F in the oven.
2. In a large skillet, warm the oil over medium to high heat. Put in the onion, garlic, basil, carrot, and thyme. Add the meat, cook it for 1-2 minutes, and then break up any clumps with a spatula.
3. Add the zucchini, parsley, and kidney beans for 5 to 6 minutes after the beef begins to brown.
4. When prepping peppers, cut the tops off slightly above the roots
5. You should remove the pulp and the seeds. The peppers are done when a fork can be inserted into them easily yet gently after 20–25 minutes in an oven with the foil covering the pan.
6. In a small casserole, heat the marinara sauce, and before serving, pour over each plated bell pepper.

Nutritional value per serving:

Calories 443, Total Fat 22 grams, Saturated Fat 6 grams, Polyunsaturated Fat 2 grams, Monounsaturated Fat 10 grams, Cholesterol 43 mg, Sodium 988 mg, Potassium 937 mg, Total Carbohydrate 46 grams, Dietary Fiber 12 grams, Sugars 13 grams, Protein 20 grams.

Sesame Salmon Fillets

Makes two servings

Ingredients:

- One tablespoon of sesame oil
- 2 (4-ounce) salmon fillets, skin on
- 1/8 teaspoon ground ginger
- 1/8 teaspoon sea salt
- 1/8 teaspoon cracked black pepper
- Two teaspoons of black sesame seeds

How to make:

1. Heat the oil in a medium oven. Use ginger powder, salt, pepper, and sesame seeds to cover each fillet. Softly pat the roots down, so they adhere to the filet. Turn the fillets over after around 3 to 4 minutes, and then scan the other side. Lift the fillets from the pan after 1 to 2 minutes, and serve immediately.

2. Serving Suggestion: Serve with broccoli or sautéed vegetables and whole couscous wheat.

Nutritional value:

Fat 9 grams, Monounsaturated Fat 7 grams, Cholesterol 81 mg, Sodium 204 mg, Potassium 756 mg, Total Carbohydrate 2 grams, Dietary Fiber 1 gram, Sugars 0.1 grams, Protein 31 grams

Spice-Rubbed Salmon

Makes four servings

Ingredients:

- Two teaspoons of chili powder
- One teaspoon of ground cumin
- One teaspoon of brown sugar
- 1/8 teaspoon sea salt
- 1/8 teaspoon cracked black pepper
- 4 (4-ounce) salmon fillets
- Juice of 1/2 orange
- Two tablespoons of extra virgin olive oil

How to make

1. Blend the chili powder, cumin, sugar, salt, and pepper in a small bowl. Rub the mixture by hand onto every salmon filet.

2. Heat the oil. Once the oil is hot, add two fillets to the pan at a time, skin side down, and cook well for 3 minutes. Turn over the fillets, then squeeze orange juice over them. Cook for another 3 minutes, until the fillets are flaky and, with a fork, can be removed. Repeat with a second set of filets the method. Serve straight away.

Nutritional value per serving

Calories 295, Total Fat 18 grams, Saturated Fat 3 grams, Polyunsaturated Fat 5 grams, Monounsaturated Fat 9 grams, Cholesterol 81 mg, Sodium 78 mg, Potassium 776 mg, Total Carbohydrate 3 grams, Dietary Fiber 0.9 grams, Sugars 2 grams, Protein 29 grams.

Pan-Steamed Orange Roughy

Makes four servings

Ingredients:

- Four small green onions, white ends cut off
- Four teaspoons of chopped fresh ginger
- 4 (3-ounce) orange rough fillets

- Three large cloves of garlic, minced
- 1/4 teaspoon cracked black pepper
- 1/2 teaspoon black sesame seeds
- One lime, very thinly sliced
- Two teaspoons of sesame oil

How to make

1. Cut four foil pieces, roughly six by 6 inches. Place a green onion in the center of each board, along with one teaspoon of ginger. Sprinkle with garlic, pepper, and sesame seeds, and put one fillet on top. Place four slices of paper-thin lime on top of each fillet, and drizzle with the oil. Wrap each filet by folding up the foil from the sides, meet in the middle and fold down to seal.

2. Set over medium-high, set a large flat pan, and put the foil-wrapped fillets in the oven. Cook for eight to 10 minutes.

3. Remove the fish packages from the pan and sit in the foil for 3 to 4 minutes to keep steaming. Serve in the foil so that everyone can unwrap their meal.

Nutritional value per serving:

Polyunsaturated Fat 1 gram, Monounsaturated Fat 2 g, Cholesterol 22 mg, Sodium 74 mg, Potassium 438 mg, Total Carbohydrate 5 grams, Dietary Fiber 1 gram, Sugars 1 gram, Protein 17 grams.

Fish Tacos

Makes four servings

Ingredients:

- 4 (3-ounce) Mahi Mahi fillets
- Three tablespoons of extra virgin olive oil
- 4 cups thinly shredded red cabbage
- Two large avocados, pitted, peeled, and thinly sliced
- Three large Roma tomatoes, chopped
- Three tablespoons of red wine vinegar
- Eight corn tortillas
- 1/2 teaspoon ground cumin
- 1/8 teaspoon cracked black pepper
- For sauce;
- 3/4 cup low-fat plain Greek yogurt
- 1/4 cup of low-fat milk
- Juice of 1 large lemon
- 1/8 teaspoon cracked black pepper
- 1/8 teaspoon sea salt

How to make

1. To make the sauce, whisk all ingredients together in a small bowl. The thickness of the pizza sauce should be relatively thin to drizzle over the top of the tacos, adding more milk if it isn't light enough. Set aside.

2. Heat a large pan over medium heat. Season both sides with cumin and pepper. Cook each side until each side is seared and the middle of the fish is no longer translucent. Remove from the oven, and clean on paper

towels. Repeat with the other two fillets.

3. In a separate bowl, mix the cabbage with the vinegar. Using two forks, split apart each fillet into two parts. Warm the tortillas in a flat pan on low heat, then put a couple of pieces of fish in each tortilla, top with the cabbage mixture, avocado, and chopped tomato, and then drizzle with sauce. Fold the tortilla and serve.

Nutritional value per serving:

Calories 483, Total Fat 29 grams, Saturated Fat 4 grams, Polyunsaturated Fat 4 grams, Monounsaturated Fat 17 grams, Cholesterol 137 mg, Sodium 323 mg, Potassium 1,145 mg, Total Carbohydrate 48 grams, Dietary Fiber 14 grams, Sugars 6 grams, Protein 43 grams.

Thai Curried Vegetables

Makes four servings

Ingredients:

- Two large cloves of garlic, coarsely chopped
- One teaspoon of curry powder
- 1/2 teaspoon ground cinnamon
- 1/2 teaspoon ground turmeric
- 1/2 teaspoon cracked black pepper
- Two tablespoons of coconut oil
- One medium onion, cut into 1/4-inch pieces
- One medium red bell pepper, coarsely chopped
- One medium green bell pepper, coarsely chopped
- 1 cup coarsely chopped broccoli
- 3–4 cups cubed eggplant, 1/2-inch pieces
- One small jalapeño Chile pepper, thinly sliced (seeded for less heat)
- One tablespoon of chopped fresh ginger
- 2 cups unsweetened light coconut milk
- 1/2 cup low-sodium vegetable broth
- One heaping tablespoon of unsalted peanut butter
- Four tablespoons of coarsely chopped Thai basil

How to make

1. Steam in a large pot over medium heat, and add coconut oil.

2. Stirring constantly after it has cooled, add the onion, bell peppers, and broccoli. Remove eggplant, chili pepper, ginger, garlic, curry powder, turmeric, cinnamon, and pepper. Stir in the ingredients and spices, and cook until brown eggplant and vegetables soften, around 4 to 5 minutes. Add the butter with coconut milk, broth, and peanut. Stir well to bring in the peanut butter, then cover the pot.

3. Simmer on low for 10 minutes or so. Then

remove the lid and cook for another 5 minutes, uncovered or until the sauce thickens to the desired consistency; right before serving, mix in the basil.

4. Serving Suggestion: In individual bowls, scoop 1/2 cup of cooked brown rice, and top each with a large spoon of veggies and sauce.

5. Fun Fact: Thai basil has a more robust flavor than Italian basil, with an undertone of licorice.

Nutritional value per serving:

Calories 270, Total Fat 21 grams, Saturated Fat 18 grams, Polyunsaturated Fat 0.4 gram, Monounsaturated Fat 0.5 grams, Cholesterol 0 mg, Sodium 107 mg, Potassium 441 mg, Total Carbohydrate 16 grams, Dietary Fiber 5 grams, Sugars 2 grams, Protein 6 grams

Veggie Fajitas

Makes four servings

Ingredients:

- Three large red bell peppers, cut into strips
- Three large green bell peppers, cut into strips
- Three large yellow bell peppers, cut into strips
- Two large green zucchini, cut into strips
- Two large portobello mushrooms about 6 inches in diameter
- Two large white onions, sliced
- Three tablespoons of extra virgin olive oil
- Three cloves of garlic, minced
- 1 1/2 teaspoons dried oregano
- 1/4 teaspoon ground cumin
- 1/8 teaspoon cracked black pepper
- 1/8 teaspoon sea salt
- Eight corn tortillas

How to make

1. Cut each bell pepper in half lengthwise. The zucchini should be sliced lengthwise into thin strips, and each strip should be halved. After wiping them down with a damp cloth, popping off the stem ends, and picking out the gills with a spoonful of metal, the mushrooms are ready to be sliced into half-inch strips.

Slice the onions into half-centimeter-thick pieces.

2. To prepare the oil, place it in a large pot and heat it over medium-high heat. Once the oil is hot, add the vegetables and seasonings (peppers, zucchini, mushrooms, onions, garlic, orégano, cumin, pepper, salt). Warm everything up in a pan for around 5–6 minutes or until the onions are transparent and the vegetables are tender.

3. Warm the tortillas in a flat pan over medium heat, and spoon in the veggies. Fold over the tortilla, and serve.

4. Serving Suggestion: Serve with black beans

and be imaginative with toppings, such as plain Greek yogurt (instead of sour cream), salsa, shredded lettuce, guacamole, or low-fat shredded cheese.

Nutritional value per serving:

Calories 343, Total Fat 13 grams, Saturated Fat 2 grams, Polyunsaturated Fat 8 grams, Monounsaturated Fat 8 grams, Cholesterol 0 mg, Sodium 89 mg, Potassium 795 mg, Total Carbohydrate 55 grams, Dietary Fiber 14 grams, Sugars 7 grams, protein 12 grams.

Grilled Portobello Burger with Caramelized Onions and Pesto

Makes four servings

Ingredients:

- Four medium portobello mushrooms (about 4 inches in diameter)
- Four tablespoons of extra virgin olive oil
- 1/4 teaspoon sea salt
- 1/2 teaspoon ground black pepper
- Eight tablespoons of balsamic vinegar
- 4 100% whole wheat hamburger buns
- Four tablespoons of prepared pesto
- Four tablespoons of Caramelized Onions

How to make

1. Clean the mushrooms.
2. Remove the stems of the mushroom and scoop the brown gills with a metal spoon, then discard. Brush each mushroom with a spoonful of oil and sprinkle with salt, pepper, and two tablespoons of balsamic vinegar on the inside of each mushroom. Set aside for 20 minutes minimum.
3. Place the mushrooms, top-down, on a hot grill or grill pan.
4. Grill for 5 to 7 minutes, then grill for another 5 to 7 minutes or until tender. Do not treat them too much to prevent the release of the juices.
5. Toast the buns while the mushrooms grill for about 1 minute by putting them face down on the grill. Remove from the grill, and spread one spoonful of pesto inside each top bun. Place one mushroom on the bottom of each bun, then top with one tablespoon of caramelized onions.

Nutritional value per serving:

Calories 424, Total Fat 25 grams, Saturated Fat 4 grams, Polyunsaturated Fat 3 grams, Monounsaturated Fat 10 grams, Cholesterol 0 mg, Sodium 607 mg, Potassium 40 mg, Total Carbohydrate 45 grams, Dietary Fiber 6 grams, Sugars 6 grams, Protein 10 grams.

Caramelized Onions

Makes ten servings

Ingredients:

- Two tablespoons of extra virgin olive oil
- 4 cups thinly sliced white onions
- One teaspoon of brown sugar
- 1/8 teaspoon cracked black pepper

How to make

1. Place a saucepan of medium size over medium heat. Add the oil, onions, sugar, and pepper if the oil is hot. Stir in for 5 to 10 minutes, continually stirring to avoid burning. Once the onions become translucent and begin to turn brown, cover the pan and turn the heat low. Let "sweat" the onions for another 5 minutes. They should be dark brown when done and very delicate.

Nutritional value per serving:

Calories 43, Total Fat 3 grams, Saturated Fat.04 grams, Polyunsaturated Fat.04 grams, Monounsaturated Fat 2 grams, Cholesterol 0 mg, Sodium 2 mg, Potassium 74 mg, Total Carbohydrate 5 grams, Dietary Fiber.08 grams, Sugars.06 grams, Protein.05 gram

Mediterranean Bowl

Makes four servings

- 1 cup uncooked whole wheat couscous
- 1 1/4 cups of water
- 1 (16-ounce) can of artichoke hearts
- 1/2 cup rinsed, drained, and pitted kalamata olives
- 1 (12-ounce) jar of roasted red peppers, rinsed, drained, and coarsely chopped
- 1/2 cup low-fat feta cheese
- 1 cup chopped cherry tomatoes
- 1/2 small red onion, finely diced
- 1/4 teaspoon finely chopped fresh oregano
- 1/4 teaspoon finely chopped fresh mint
- Pinch of chile pepper flakes
- Four tablespoons of extra virgin olive oil
- Juice of 1 lemon
- Cracked black pepper

How to make

1. Boil the water, add the couscous, stir, and turn off the heat.
2. Cover the pot with a lid, sit for 5 minutes before serving, and fluff it with a fork.
3. Combine all ingredients, except for the cooked couscous, and mix well. Refrigerate in the couscous for 15 to 20 minutes, then fold in. Serve at room temperature or cold.
4. Suggestion: Great with salmon fillets, chicken breasts, or chicken or tuna salad mixed in.

Advice: • The brining liquid in which many jarred olives are preserved is rather salty. To reduce the amount of salt in the olives, rinse and drain them.

Per-serving nutritional value

Including the fat and carbs, this dish has a calorie count of 433 (50% from fat), a total fat count of 20 (50% Polyunsaturated Fat 3 g, Monounsaturated Fat 12 g, Cholesterol 17 mg, Sodium 432 mg, Potassium 513 mg, Total Carbohydrate 54 g, Dietary Fiber 12 g, Sugars 0 g, Protein 13 g

Grilled Veggie Pizza

Makes six servings

- Two medium portobello mushrooms about 4 inches in diameter
- One small yellow zucchini, cut in half lengthwise
- One small red onion, cut into rounds
- 1/8 teaspoon cracked black pepper
- 1 (1-pound) whole-wheat pizza dough
- Two plum tomatoes, thinly sliced
- 1/2 cup shredded skim mozzarella cheese
- 1/4 cup fresh basil leaves, coarsely chopped
- Four tablespoons of extra-virgin olive oil
- 1/8 teaspoon salt

How to make

1. Preheat to 400 ° F in the oven.
2. Heat over medium heat to a grill or grill pan. Wipe the mushrooms with a damp towel, snap off the stems, scoop out the gills with a tablespoon of metal, and cut them into 1/2-inch strips.
3. Brush with two tablespoons of oil the mushrooms, zucchini, and onion, and sprinkle on salt and pepper. Cook the vegetables for around 6 minutes on the grill., rotating once, until tender and brown. Remove the onion rings from the grill, and separate them.
4. Coat a cookie sheet with a spray of olive oil. Stretch the pizza dough onto the cookie sheet with your fingertips, or roll the dough out onto a floured surface to prevent sticking. For best baking results, prick the dough with a fork. Roll out the dough and rub in the last two tablespoons of olive oil. Spread with your fingers or a spatula, and bake for 12 to 15 minutes or until crispy.
5. Remove from the oven the pizza crust, and quickly top with vegetables and cheese. Exit the range for 5 to 6 minutes until the cheese melts.
6. Remove from the frying pan, cover with basil and serve.
7. RECIPE ALTERATIONS • Top the marinara sauce with low-sodium dough before baking for a different flavor.
8. Turn up the vegetables or add more vegetables.
9. Split the dough in half if you prefer pizza with a thin crust.

10. The pizza crust is pre-cooked and works well. Just look for the entire wheat crust at 100 percent.

Nutritional value per serving

Calories 159, Total Fat 6 grams, Saturated Fat 2 grams, Polyunsaturated Fat 0.5 grams, Monounsaturated Fat 3 grams, Cholesterol 11 mg, Sodium 299 mg, Potassium 112 mg, Total Carbohydrate 18 grams, Dietary Fiber 3 grams, Sugars 0.5 grams, Protein 8 grams.

Berry Muesli

- One cup old-fashioned rolled oats (raw)
- One cup fruit yogurt
- 1/2 cup 1% milk
- Pinch of salt
- 1/2 cup dried fruit (try raisins, apricots, dates)
- 1/2 cup chopped apple
- 1/2 cup frozen blueberries
- 1/4 cup chopped, toasted walnuts

Directions:

1. In a medium bowl, mix oats, yogurt, milk, and salt.
2. Cover and refrigerate for 6-12 hours.
3. Add dried and fresh fruit, and mix gently.
4. Serve scoops of muesli in small dishes. Sprinkle each serving with chopped nuts.
5. Refrigerate leftovers within 2-3 hours.

Tips:

Prepare this recipe the night before and enjoy a balanced breakfast that is sure to keep you full until lunch because it is a good source of fiber. This dish also contains antioxidants and omega 3s.

Veggie Quiche Muffins

- 3/4 cup low-fat cheddar cheese, shredded
- One cup green onion or onion, chopped
- One cup broccoli, chopped
- One cup tomato, diced
- 2 cups non-fat or 1% milk
- Four eggs
- One cup baking mix (for biscuits or pancakes)
- One teaspoon Italian seasoning (or dried leaf basil and oregano)
- 1/2 teaspoon salt
- 1/2 teaspoon pepper

Directions:

1. Heat oven to 375 degrees. Lightly spray or oil 12 muffin cups.
2. Sprinkle cheese, onions, broccoli, and tomatoes

in muffin cups.

3. Place remaining ingredients in a bowl and beat until smooth. Pour egg mixture over other ingredients into muffin cups.

4. Bake until golden brown or until knife inserted in center comes out clean, 35-40 minutes. Cool, five minutes.

5. Refrigerate leftovers within 2 hours.

Tips:

Get creative and try different types of low-fat cheeses. Also, consider using spinach, mushrooms, bell peppers, and even jalapenos for extra nutrients and a colorful muffin. Try pairing this with whole-grain toast for a great breakfast.

Turkey Sausage and Mushroom Strata

- Eight ounces wheat ciabatta bread cut into 1-inch cubes
- 12 ounces turkey sausage (can be found in the frozen section)
- Two cups fat free milk
- 1-1/2 cup (4 ounces) reduced-fat shredded sharp cheddar cheese
- Three large eggs
- 12 ounces egg substitute
- ½ cup chopped green onion
- 1 cup sliced mushrooms
- ½ teaspoon paprika
- Fresh ground pepper to taste
- Two tablespoons grated parmesan cheese

Directions:

1. Preheat oven to 400°.

2. Arrange bread cubes on a baking sheet. Bake at 400° for for eight minutes or until toasted.

3. Heat a medium skillet over medium-high heat. Add sausage to pan; cook 7 minutes or until browned, stirring to crumble.

4. Combine milk, cheese, eggs, egg substitute, parmesan cheese, paprika, salt and pepper in a large bowl, stirring with a whisk.

5. Add bread, sausage, scallions and mushrooms, tossing well to coat bread. Spoon mixture into a 13×9-inch baking dish. Cover and refrigerate eight hours or overnight.

6. Preheat the oven to 350°.

7. Uncover casserole. Bake at 350° for 50 minutes or until set and lightly browned. Cut into 12 pieces; serve immediately.

Tips:

Whole wheat bread adds fiber and nutrients, both of which are heart healthy, to this otherwise simple breakfast casserole. Serve with fresh apple slices and a glass of hot chocolate for a satisfying cold weather breakfast.

Sweet Millet Congee

- Eight strips of bacon
- One cup hulled millet
- Five cups water
- 1 cup sweet potato, peeled and diced
- 2 teaspoons ginger, minced (optional)
- One teaspoon ground cinnamon
- 2 Tablespoons brown sugar
- One medium apple, diced with skin
- ¼ cup honey

Directions:

1. Cook bacon in a skillet over medium-high heat until crispy. Remove from pan and blot with a paper towel to remove excess fat. Once cooled, crumble bacon strips and set aside.
2. Rinse and drain millet.
3. Combine millet, water, sweet potato, ginger, cinnamon, and brown sugar in a deep pot. Bring to a boil, reduce heat to low and simmer, stirring often, until water is absorbed (about one hour).
4. Once millet is cooked, remove pot from heat and add apple, honey and bacon crumbles.
5. Slow cooker method: Reduce water by one cup and cook on high for two to 2 ½ hours.

Tips:

Congee is a porridge made with rice or millet and is popular in many Asian countries. This hearty, whole grain breakfast is a perfect make ahead meal. Make a batch at the beginning of the week, portion into eight single serving microwave safe containers and store in the refrigerator. Now all you need to do each morning is pop it in the microwave for one minute (or until hot) and enjoy a healthy breakfast every day this week! If the congee is too thick once reheated, add a splash of nonfat milk.

Sweet Millet Congee

- Eight strips of bacon
- One cup hulled millet
- Five cups water
- One cup sweet potato, peeled and diced
- 2 teaspoons ginger, minced (optional)
- One teaspoon ground cinnamon
- 2 Tablespoons brown sugar
- One medium apple, diced with skin
- ¼ cup honey

Directions:

1. Cook bacon in a skillet over medium-high heat until crispy. Remove from pan and blot with a paper towel to remove excess fat. Once cooled, crumble bacon strips and set aside.
2. Rinse and drain millet.
3. Combine millet, water, sweet potato, ginger, cinnamon and brown sugar in a deep pot. Bring to a boil, reduce heat to low and simmer, stirring often, until water is absorbed (about 1 hour).
4. Once millet is cooked, remove pot from heat

and add apple, honey, and bacon crumbles.

5. Slow cooker method: Reduce water by 1 cup and cook on high for two to 2 ½ hours.

Tips:

Congee is a porridge made with rice or millet and is popular in many Asian countries. This hearty, whole grain breakfast is a perfect make ahead meal. Make a batch at the beginning of the week, portion into eight single serving microwave safe containers and store in the refrigerator. Now all you need to do each morning is pop it in the microwave for one minute (or until hot) and enjoy a healthy breakfast every day this week! If the congee is too thick once reheated, add a splash of nonfat milk.

Summer Quinoa Bowls

- 1 small peach, sliced
- 1/3 cup uncooked quinoa, rinsed well
- 2/3 + 3/4 cup low-fat milk
- 1/2 teaspoon vanilla extract
- Two teaspoons brown sugar
- 12 raspberries
- blueberries
- Two teaspoons honey

Directions:

1. In sauce pan combine quinoa and 2/3 cup milk, vanilla, and brown sugar.

2. Cook on medium heat and bring to boil for five minutes. Reduce heat to low and cover. Cook for 15 to 20 minutes, or until easily fluffs with a fork.

3. Meanwhile, heat a grill pan and spray with oil. Grill the peaches to bring out their sweetness two to three minutes; set aside. Warm the remaining milk in the microwave.

4. Divide the cooked quinoa between two bowls then pour in warmed milk. Top with peaches, raspberries and blueberries and drizzle each with one teaspoon of honey.

Tips:

This protein-rich breakfast also packs in Calcium, Potassium, Vitamin A, and antioxidants. To add in more nutrients, try nuts or sneak in ground flax seeds to increase the omega-3 content. This recipe was slightly changed from its original version which is called for almond beverage to including low-fat cow's milk. This increased the protein content to 11 g while increasing the Potassium content, both important characteristics for the DASH diet.

Strawberry Sandwich (Halves)

- 8 ounces Neufchatel cheese or low-fat cream cheese, softened
- One tablespoon honey
- One teaspoon grated Lemon zest
- 4 English muffins, split and toasted
- Two cups (about 10 ounces) sliced

strawberries

Directions:

1. In food processor, process cheese, honey and zest until well mixed, or mix in bowl with wooden spoon.

2. Spread one tablespoon cheese mixture on cut side of 1 muffin half; top with one-quarter cup strawberries.

3. Repeat with remaining ingredients to make eight half-sandwiches.

Tips:

Don't feel limited to strawberries- make it more colorful with raspberries and blueberries while packing in the antioxidants! Add in nuts, and seeds for a nice crunch and consider using low-sodium, low-fat cottage cheese instead of cream cheese for a sweet-and-salty flavor.

Steel Cut Oat Blueberry Pancakes

- 1-1/2 cups water
- ½ cup steel cut oats
- 1/8 teaspoon sea salt
- One cup whole wheat flour
- ½ teaspoon baking powder
- ½ teaspoon baking soda
- One egg
- One cup milk
- ½ cup Greek yogurt, vanilla flavor
- 1 cup frozen blueberries
- ½ cup + 2 tablespoons agave nectar

Directions:

1. In a medium pot bring water to a boil and add steel cut oats and salt. Reduce heat to a low simmer and cook until oats are tender, about ten minutes. Remove from heat and set aside.

2. In a medium mixing, bowl combine whole wheat pastry flour, baking powder and soda, egg, milk and yogurt. Mix until a batter is formed. Gently folds in blueberries and cooked oats.

3. Heat griddle or non-stick skillet heated over medium and coat with cooking spray. Spoon one quarter cup of batter onto surface and cook until pancakes begin to bubble and are slightly golden, about 2 – 3 minutes per side, working in batches if needed.

4. 4. Garnish each pancake with about one tablespoon agave nectar.

Tips:

For an additional twist to this already delicious meal, try adding different berries, apple sauce or mixed nuts to create an other meal every morning. Add cinnamon or nutmeg to boost the flavor. A glass of nonfat milk will add protein and help meet your daily DASH goals.

Spinach, Mushroom, and Feta Cheese Scramble

- Cooking spray
- ½ cup fresh mushrooms, sliced
- 1 cup fresh spinach, chopped
- One whole egg and two egg whites
- 2 tablespoons feta cheese
- Pepper to taste

Directions:

1. Heat an 8-inch non-stick sauté pan over medium heat. Spray with cooking spray and add mushrooms and spinach.
2. Sauté mushrooms and spinach for 2-3 minutes or until the spinach has wilted.
3. Whisk the egg and egg whites in a bowl with feta cheese and pepper if desired. Pour egg mixture over vegetables in the pan.
4. Continue to cook eggs while stirring with a spatula for another 3-4 minutes or until the eggs are cooked through.

Tips:

This recipe is an easy way to add some fresh vegetables to your day. Get creative and throw in some fresh bell peppers, green onions, or tomatoes. You can also try using fresh grated parmesan cheese instead of feta.

Refrigerator Overnight Oatmeal

- 1 cup old fashion oatmeal, uncooked
- One cup nonfat vanilla yogurt
- ½ cup non-fat milk
- 1 cup frozen blueberries
- 1 Tablespoon chia seeds

Directions:

- Place all ingredients in a mixing bowl and mix well.
- Spoon the oatmeal mixture into two small containers and cover with a fitted lid. Place in the refrigerator.
- Let the oatmeal sit overnight in the refrigerator. Enjoy your overnight oatmeal the next morning as a cold breakfast treat.

Tips:

This tasty, high-fiber breakfast is sure to keep you full all morning. The milk and yogurt give the oats the moisture they need to soften making this the perfect no bake breakfast recipe. To keep your mornings interesting swap out the frozen blueberries for your favorite fruit. Try replacing the blueberries for ½ cup frozen strawberries and top with half of a sliced banana right before you eat. You can even add a tablespoon of cocoa powder to turn your oatmeal into a chocolate delight.

Red Velvet Pancakes with Cream Cheese Topping

- *Cream Cheese Topping:*
- 2 ounces 1/3 less fat cream cheese
- Three tablespoons plain fat free yogurt
- Three tablespoons honey
- One tablespoon of fat-free milk
- *Pancakes:*
- ½ cup white whole wheat flour
- ½ cup unbleached all-purpose flour
- Two ¼ teaspoons of baking powder
- ½ tablespoon unsweetened cocoa powder
- ¼ teaspoon salt
- ¼ cup sugar
- One large egg
- 1 cup + 2 tablespoons fat-free milk
- One teaspoon vanilla
- ½ teaspoon red paste food coloring

Directions:

- Combine the cream cheese topping ingredients, and set aside.
- Mix the flours, baking powder, cocoa powder, sugar, and salt in a large bowl.
- In another dissolve the food coloring with the milk; whisk in egg and vanilla.
- Combine wet and dry ingredients until there are no more dry spots, careful not to overmix.
- Heat a large non-stick griddle pan on medium-low heat. When hot, lightly spray with oil to coat and pour ¼ cup of the pancake batter onto the pan.
- When the pancake starts to bubble and the edges begin to set, flip the pancakes. Repeat with the remainder of the batter.
- To serve, place two pancakes on each plate, then top with about 2 ½ tablespoons of the cream cheese topping.

Tips:

Using plain fat-free yogurt and fat-free milk are a great way to lighten up the cream cheese topping in this recipe. If you are watching your added sugar content you a sweetener of your choice, such as Splenda or Stevia, would work in place of sugar.

Perfect Granola

- ¼ cup canola oil
- Four tablespoons honey
- 1 ½ teaspoons vanilla
- 6 c rolled oats (old fashioned)
- One cup almond, slivered
- ½ cup unsweetened coconut, shredded
- Two cups bran flakes
- 3/4 cup walnuts, chopped

- 1 cup raisins
- Cooking spray or parchment paper

Directions:

1. Preheat oven to 325 degrees.
2. Place oil, honey and vanilla in a small saucepan. Cook gently over low heat, stirring occasionally for five minutes or until combined.
3. Place remaining ingredients, except the raisins, in a large mixing bowl and mix well. Slowly stir in the oil-honey mixture, making sure that grains are evenly coated.
4. Lightly sprays a baking tray with cooking spray or cover with parchment paper. Spread the cereal over the baking tray and bake in the oven for 25 minutes, or until the grains are crisp and very lightly browned. Stir occasionally to prevent the mixture from burning.
5. Remove the cereal from the oven and allow it to cool. Add raisins and stir evenly through the grain mixture.

    Serving size: about ½ cup

Tips:

This granola is rich in fiber and heart healthy oils. Layer with low fat yogurt and fresh berries for a delicious, well-balanced breakfast parfait.

Peanut Butter & Banana Smoothie

- 1 cup nonfat milk
- One tablespoon of all natural peanut butter
- 1 medium banana, frozen or fresh

Directions:

Combine all ingredients in a blender, and blend until very smooth.

Tips:

With the potassium provided by the non-fat milk and the banana in this simple breakfast, this recipe is a Dash diet dream!

1) PB + J Yogurt

- 6 ounces fat free plain Greek yogurt
- Four teaspoons reduced sugar grape jelly
- Two tablespoons red seedless grapes cut in half
- One tablespoon reduced-fat peanut butter
- One teaspoon unsalted peanuts

Directions:

1. Place the yogurt in a bowl.
2. Top with jelly, then peanut butter.
3. Then lightly sprinkle peanuts and grapes over the top of the yogurt.

Tips:

The combination of the Greek yogurt mixed with peanuts and peanut butter gives you a perfect mixture of fats and protein that will you leave you full and satisfied enough to get through the morning.

Overnight Oatmeal

- 4 cups of fat-free milk
- 4 cups water
- Two cups steel-cut oats
- 1/3 cup raisins
- 1/3 cup dried cherries
- 1/3 cup dried apricots, chopped
- One teaspoon molasses
- 1 teaspoon cinnamon (or pumpkin pie spice)

Directions:

1. In a slow cooker, combine all of the ingredients.
2. Turn heat to low. Put the lid on and cook overnight for 8 to 9 hours.
3. Spoon into bowls and serve.

Tips:

Steel-cut oats, also known as oat groats or Irish oats, are whole grain oats that have been cut into two or three pieces. Eating whole grains, like oats, can reduce the risk of coronary heart disease and help you meet the DASH goal of making half your grains whole. If this recipe makes more then you need you can store leftovers in the refrigerator and re-heat as needed throughout the week.

No Bake Granola Bars

- 2 1/2 cups toasted rice cereal
- Two cups old fashioned oatmeal
- 1/2 cup raisins
- 1/2 cup firmly packed brown sugar
- 1/2 cup light corn syrup
- 1/2 cup peanut butter
- One teaspoon vanilla

Directions:

1. Combine rice cereal, oatmeal, and raisins in a large mixing bowl and stir together with a wooden spoon.
2. In a 1-quart saucepan, mix together brown sugar and corn syrup. Turn the heat to medium-high. Stir constantly while the mixture is brought to a boil. Once boiling, remove the saucepan from the heat.
3. Stir the peanut butter and vanilla into the sugar mixture in the saucepan. Blend until smooth.
4. Pour the peanut butter mixture over the cereal and raisins in the mixing bowl. Mix well.
5. Press the mixture into a 9 x 13 baking pan. Let cool completely and cut into 18 bars.

Tips:

Pack with a one cup container of yogurt and a piece of fruit to make it a portable meal.

Mushroom Shallot Frittata

- One tablespoon of unsalted butter

- Four shallots, finely chopped
- ½ pounds mushrooms, finely chopped
- Two teaspoons fresh parsley, chopped
- One teaspoon dried thyme
- Black pepper to taste
- Three eggs
- Five large egg whites
- One tablespoon milk or fat-free half and half
- ¼ cup fresh parmesan cheese, grated

Directions:

1. Preheat oven to 350 degrees.
2. Heat butter in a large ovenproof skillet over medium heat. Stir in shallots and sauté until golden, about 5 minutes. Add chopped mushroom, parsley, thyme and black pepper.
3. In a medium bowl whisk eggs, egg whites, parmesan, and milk. Add the egg mixture to the skillet, making sure eggs cover all the mushrooms. When the edges begin to set (about two minutes) move the skillet to the oven. Bake for about 15 minutes, or until frittata is completely cooked.
4. Serve warm, cut into four equal wedges.

Tips:

Serve with whole grain bread, fresh fruit, and a cold glass of milk for a well-balanced and nutrient-rich meal. Frittatas aren't only for breakfast and brunch – they pair wonderfully with salads for lunch or dinner.

Morning Quinoa

- Two cups low fat or nonfat milk
- One cup uncooked quinoa
- ¼ cup honey or brown sugar
- ¼ teaspoon cinnamon, plus more to taste
- ¼ cup sliced or slivered almonds
- ¼ cup dried currants, chopped dried apricots, or fresh berries

Directions:

1. Rinse the quinoa thoroughly.
2. Bring the milk to a boil in a medium saucepan. Add the quinoa and return to a boil.
3. Cover, reduce heat to medium-low, and simmer until most of the liquid is absorbed (about 12-15 minutes).
4. Remove from heat and fluff with a fork. Stir in remaining ingredients, cover, and let stand for 15 minutes.

Tips:

This one-dish breakfast is gluten free and a great source of protein and calcium. Add extra milk for a thinner consistency and extra calcium!

Jack-o-Lantern Pancakes

- One egg
- ½ cup canned pumpkin
- One ¾ cups low-fat milk

- Two tablespoons of vegetable oil
- 2 cups flour
- Two tablespoons brown sugar
- One tablespoon baking powder
- 1 teaspoon pumpkin pie spice
- One teaspoon salt

Directions:

1. Combine eggs, pumpkin, milk and oil in large mixing bowl.
2. Add flour, brown sugar, baking powder, pumpkin pie spice, and salt to egg mixture. Stir gently.
3. Lightly coat a griddle or skillet with cooking spray and heat on medium.
4. Using a ¼ cup measure, pour batter on hot griddle. Cook until bubbles begin to burst, flip over, then cook until golden brown.

Optional: Put a face on the jack-o-lantern, using raisins for eyes and teeth (drop in batter while it cooks).

Tips:

Replace the vegetable oil with applesauce to cut calories, and use whole-wheat flour instead of white flour to add fiber, vitamins, and minerals.

Fruit-n-Grain Breakfast Salad

- Three cups water
- ¼ tsp salt
- ¾ cup quick-cooking brown rice
- ¾ cup bulgur
- 1 Granny Smith apple
- 1 Red Delicious apple
- One orange
- One cup raisins
- One container (8 oz) low-fat vanilla yogurt

Directions:

1. In a large pot, heat water and salt to boiling over high heat.
2. Add rice and bulgur, reduce heat to low, cover, and cook for ten minutes.
3. Remove from heat and set aside, covered 2 minutes.
4. Spread hot grains on baking sheet to cool (this will make them fluffier). Grains can be prepared the night before and kept in the refrigerator.
5. Just before serving, prepare fruit: core and chop apples. Peel orange and cut into sections.
6. Transfer the chilled grains and cut fruit to a medium mixing bowl. Stir the yogurt into the grains and fruit until coated.

Tips:

Three different fruit, cooked whole grains and lowfat yogurt make this salad is a perfect DASH breakfast. The yogurt's protein and fiber from the whole grains and fruit will keep you feeling satisfied all morning.

Fruit Pizza

- 1 English Muffin (try the whole grain)
- Two tablespoons reduced fat or fat-free cream cheese (see notes)
- Two tablespoons sliced strawberries
- Two tablespoons blueberries
- Two tablespoons crushed pineapple

Directions:

1. Split open the English muffin and toast the halves until lightly browned.
2. Spread cream cheese on both halves.
3. Divide the fruit between the two muffins halves and arrange on top of cream cheese.
4. These is best when served soon.
5. Refrigerate leftovers within two hours.

Tips:

Fruit pizzas are perfect for a quick breakfast, afterschool snack, or dessert. Each mouthwatering pizza packs a nutritious punch with fiber, protein, and vitamins.

Flax Banana Yogurt Muffins

1 cup whole wheat flour

- One cup old-fashioned rolled oats
- One teaspoon baking soda
- Two tablespoons ground flaxseed
- Three large bananas, mashed (~1.5 cups)
- ½ cup plain, 0% fat greek yogurt
- ¼ cup unsweetened applesauce
- ¼ cup brown sugar
- 2 teaspoon vanilla extract

Directions:

1. Preheat the oven to 355 degrees Fahrenheit
2. Prep the muffin tin with either cupcake liners or cooking spray.
3. Mix the dry ingredients in one bowl (flour, oats, soda, flaxseed).
4. Mix the wet ingredients in a separate bowl (banana, yogurt, applesauce, sugar, and vanilla)
5. Mix the dry ingredients into the wet ingredients until just combined. Batter should be lumpy. Do not over-mix.
6. Bake for 20 to 25 minutes or until a toothpick inserted into the center of a muffin comes out with crumbs, not batter.

Tips:

Nutrient-rich muffins are handy for quick breakfast. Boost protein and calcium by eating muffins with a cup of yogurt or a glass of milk.

Eggs and Tomato Breakfast Melts

- Two whole-grain English muffins, split
- One teaspoon of olive oil
- Eight egg whites, whisked
- Four scallions, finely chopped
- Kosher salt, to taste
- Black pepper, to taste
- Two ounce (about 1/2 cup) reduced-fat Swiss cheese, shredded
- 1/2 cup grape or cherry heirloom tomatoes, quartered

Directions:

1. Preheat the broiler on high. Place muffins, cut side up, on a baking sheet and broil for two minutes or until beginning to lightly brown on edges. (Or you can do this in your toaster oven)
2. Heat a medium skillet on medium heat. Add oil and sauté 3 of the scallions about 2 to 3 minutes. Add the egg whites, season with salt and pepper and cook, mixing with a wooden spoon until cooked through.
3. Divide into toasted muffins and top with tomatoes, cheese, and remaining scallions.
4. Broil for 1 to 1 1/2 minutes or until cheese has melted, careful not to burn.

Tips:

This compact breakfast item offers high-quality protein, fiber, B vitamins, vitamin C, and potassium. If you don't have whole-wheat English muffins, try other whole-grain breads or corn tortillas for a new twist.

Crunchy Avocado "Toast"

- Two brown rice cakes, unsalted
- ½ small avocado
- Small tomato, sliced
- Dried roasted red pepper flakes
- Pinch of salt

Directions:

1. Mash avocado in a bowl with a fork
2. Spread evenly over rice cakes
3. Add tomato slices as desired
4. Sprinkle with roasted red pepper flakes and pinch of salt

Tips:

Toast with jam is tasty, but sometimes the same old same old gets…well, old! Try this new rendition of your favorite breakfast go-to for a serving of heart and brain-healthy fats plus whole grains. For a protein boost, add a scrambled egg. Eat the yolk, too. There are lots of nutrients in the yolk.

Broccoli and Cheese Mini Egg Omelets

- 4 cups broccoli florets
- Four whole eggs
- One cup egg whites
- ¼ cup reduced fat cheddar
- ¼ cup grated romano or parmesan cheese

- One tablespoon olive oil
- salt and fresh pepper
- cooking spray

Directions:

1. Preheat oven to 350°F. Steam broccoli with a bit of water for about 6-7 minutes.
2. When broccoli is cooked, mash into smaller pieces and add olive oil, salt and pepper. Mix well.
3. Spray muffin tin with cooking spray and spoon broccoli mixture evenly into nine tins.
4. In a medium bowl, beat egg whites, eggs, grated parmesan cheese, salt, and pepper. Pour into the greased tins over broccoli until a little more than 3/4 full. Top with grated cheddar and bake in the oven until cooked, about 20 minutes. Serve immediately. Wrap any leftovers in plastic wrap and store in the refrigerator to enjoy during the week.

Tips:

Pair these mini-omelets with a fruit salad, whole-wheat toast, and a glass of low-fat milk and enjoy a complete well-balanced and delicious breakfast.

Breakfast Sausage, Potato and Mushroom Strata

- Eight ounces whole wheat bread, cut into one inch cube
- Six ounces of turkey or chicken breakfast sausage
- One medium russet potato (peel optional) cut into ¼-inch slices
- Two cups fat-free milk
- 1 ½ cup (4 ounces) reduced fat shredded sharp cheddar cheese
- Three large eggs
- 12 ounce egg substitute (such as Egg Beaters)
- ½ cup chopped green onions
- 1 cup sliced mushrooms
- ½ teaspoon paprika
- Dash of ground black pepper

Directions:

The night before you serve:

1. Preheat oven to 400 degrees.
2. Arrange bread cubes on a baking sheet.

3. Bake at 400° for 8 minutes or until toasted.

4. Heat a medium skillet over medium-high heat.

5. Add sausage to pan; cook seven minutes or until browned, stirring to crumble.

6. Combine milk, cheese, eggs, egg substitute, paprika and pepper in a large bowl, stirring with a whisk. Add bread, sausage, potatoes, scallions, and mushrooms, tossing well to coat bread. Spoon mixture into a 13×9-inch baking dish. Cover and refrigerate eight hours or overnight.

In the morning:

1. Preheat oven to 350°.

2. Uncover casserole.

3. Bake at 350° for 50 minutes or until set and lightly browned.

4. Cut into eight pieces; serve immediately.

Tips:

Serve with a tossed fruit salad of chopped apple, banana and oranges to add some vitamin C, potassium and color to your table this time of year!

Pumpkin Cookies

- One ¾ cups cooked, pureed pumpkin (15 ounce can)
- 1 ½ cups brown sugar
- Two eggs
- ½ cup vegetable oil
- 1 ½ cups flour
- One ¼ cups whole wheat flour
- One tablespoon baking powder
- 1 ½ teaspoon pumpkin pie spice mix
- ½ teaspoon salt
- One cup raisins
- One cup walnuts or hazelnuts, chopped

Directions:

1. Preheat oven to 400 degrees F.

2. Mix pumpkin, brown sugar, eggs, and oil thoroughly. Blend dry ingredients and add to pumpkin mixture. Add raisins and nuts.

3. Drop by teaspoonful's on greased cookie sheet, one inch apart. Gently flatten each cookie (use a spoon, bottom of glass, or palm of your hand). Bake 10-12 minutes until golden brown.

   Note: If you do not have pumpkin pie spice, use 2 teaspoons cinnamon, 1 teaspoon nutmeg, and ¼ teaspoon ground ginger.

Tips:

You can substitute raisins with golden raisins, unsweetened dried cranberries or cherries. These cookies are a great way to add a little extra fruit and nuts to your day while enjoying a DASH friendly treat.

Green Smoothie

- One medium banana
- 1 cup baby spinach, packed
- 1/2 cup fat-free milk
- 1/4 cup whole oats
- 3/4 cup frozen mango
- 1/4 cup plain nonfat yogurt
- 1/2 teaspoon vanilla

Directions:

1. Blend milk, yogurt, and oats in a blender for 15 seconds on high speed.
2. Add mango, spinach, vanilla, and banana.
3. Blend until smooth.

*Note: to add extra thickness to smoothie peel and freeze bananas the night before.

Tips:

Sometimes it can be hard to include the recommended 2-3 cups of vegetables in your diet each week. Adding spinach to a basic smoothie boosts the nutritional content without compromising taste! Spinach is a super food high in antioxidants and many important nutrients including iron, potassium, protein, and omega-3 fatty acids. Oats add an extra boost of fiber to help keep you full until lunch!

Whole Wheat Pumpkin Pancakes

- 2 ½ cups whole-wheat pastry flour
- Two tablespoons of baking powder
- Two teaspoons ground ginger
- Three teaspoons cinnamon
- ¼ teaspoon ground cloves
- ¼ teaspoon nutmeg
- Two eggs
- 2 cups low-fat buttermilk
- One cup pumpkin puree
- ¼ cup olive oil

Directions:

1. Combine the flour, baking powder, ginger, nutmeg, cinnamon, cloves, and salt in a large bowl.

2. Whisk together eggs, pumpkin puree, olive oil, and buttermilk in a separate bowl.

3. Add the wet ingredients from the second bowl to the first bowl. Mix until just incorporated.

4. Heat a skillet over medium heat. Pour ¼ cup of the pancake batter and cook until you can see small bubbles with the sides set.

5. Flip and cook until golden brown.

Tips:

Whole wheat pastry flour has more protein, fiber, and nutrients without making these pretty pancakes too dense. Instead of syrup, try serving with yogurt, warm berries, cooked apples, and/or a sprinkle of slivered almonds.

CONCLUSION

Energize yourself for the entire day with a quick breakfast sandwich or smoothie by following this fantastic diet. You'll find a long list of simple side dishes to round out the meal and DASH-friendly desserts to satisfy your sweet tooth.

Made in United States
North Haven, CT
14 January 2023

31068076R00057